Bringing In The Light

HOW TO START A LIGHTWORKER'S GROUP

Janice L. Baker, M. Ht.

This book is dedicated to all the lightworkers in our group,
past and present.

TABLE OF CONTENTS

PART THREE: THE ONGOING GROUP   94

PART FOUR: CONCLUSION   110

PART FIVE: CHECKLIST FOR GETTING STARTED   114

FOREWORD

Since November of 2009, I have been honored to share space and time with some amazing people who are all invested in making this world a better place - for all living beings. When we started there was no guidance to help us get started. There was a lot of trial and error in working things out, and a lot of lessons learned along the way. Throughout it all, we have remained focused on our mission and are loving and kind toward each other. I have learned that each person comes with a gift, whether they - or you - know what it is. There always seems to be an "aha" moment when the path for each becomes clear. It is a beautiful thing to witness. It is hoped that this book will pave the way for you to begin this work of bringing light into the world. Thank you.

ABOUT ME

It may be helpful if you know a little about me and my background and how I came to be a lightworker. After a 22 year marriage ended in 1999, I was forced to reevaluate my life and my priorities. It was no picnic, but it kicked me into gear to get going on my spiritual life. At the time I was a civil service employee working for US Fish and Wildlife Service in North Carolina. Before I retired at age 55, I began searching for the next thing I wanted to do; 55 was far too young to sit on the porch and rust. I took a number of classes before I stumbled onto hypnotherapy and knew I had found my calling. I had a private practice on the Outer Banks of North Carolina for 10 years. During that time is when I opened myself spiritually and began to explore many areas of metaphysics. I went to seminars, I read books, I meditated, I did yoga, I walked labyrinths, I did everything I could to expand my horizons and learn. The skills and knowledge I obtained along the way have been valuable to me and to our group. I consider myself still a work in progress. At the time of this writing I have moved to Santa Fe, New Mexico - far from my group - but through the miracle of technology, I am face to face with them every 2 weeks for our meetings.

BRINGING IN THE LIGHT

Welcome lightworker! If you have chosen this book, you are already a lightworker and this is just a how-to manual to put your talents to work. If you do nothing else in your life other than to shine your light, that is enough. But you want more, don't you?

In this book, I will explain, using the experiences of my own lightworker's group, how to go about beginning and maintaining a group. We have had to stumble through some of it just because there was no one to help us or give guidance; no one we knew was doing anything like this. It is the hope of our group that the experiences we have had will benefit you and help your group have a head start in moving more quickly than we did. With that being said, I do want to encourage you to take time to get a good foundation before you start doing the "heavy" work.

This book will contain narrative and also first person reports of what it is like to be in the group from an individual perspective.

Part One:

GETTING STARTED

Chapter 1:

HOW TO BEGIN

Every group seems to begin with a small gathering of like-minded individuals who want to change the world for the better. One or more of you have been labeled as over-sensitive and too far out for mainstream life. Yet, you have found each other and the ideas you toss around are not crazy in the context of your relationship with these folks. You are ready.

Janice: In 2009, I had become good friends with D and S and we spent many nights over a glass of wine talking about how to help the earth during the process of ascension to higher vibrations for people and the planet. Over several years before this, I had begun a personal journey into the metaphysical world where I finally felt at home. I didn't seem to fit into the world like other people did and had a very different perspective on what was going on in the world. 2012 was approaching and I heard all the stories about the Mayan calendar and felt strongly that it was the end of an era rather than the end of the world. I also thought that there were things that needed to be done to prepare for this transition, but had no real idea how to make that happen. One night D presented the idea to me that we should start a lightworker's group. I was very enthusiastic about the idea until he said that he wanted me to be in charge of it. That was a whole different ball game, and my initial feelings were that I was ill-prepared to take on such a job. After some discussion, I agreed. Let me add at this point that I am a hypnotherapist by trade and am comfortable taking people to a different place in their psyches and helping them feel comfortable with that process.

The next step in the process is to do a little brainstorming with these people you want to start a group with. Ideally the group should be no more than 10 people; after that it gets unwieldy. We have found the optimal group size to be from 5-9. Each of you probably know a few people that may be interested. Toss the names out to each other to assure that there is no conflict with any of the choices. If there is, I strongly suggest that you not consider that person as an invitee since group cohesion is very important. Before you take the next step of extending invitations, there needs to be a designated person in charge. By in charge, I don't mean a group dictator, but more of a group facilitator. One person needs to set meeting dates, send reminders, arrange for a meeting place, assure that there is something on the agenda for each meeting, and keep the meeting on track. That does not mean you have to do everything at every meeting. Roles will clarify as you go along, but there will always need to be a facilitator. Take a deep breath, and issue the invitations. This can be done by a face-to-face meeting or a phone call, it is more personal that way and any questions can be answered without the (sometimes) confusion of using email or message. It is important that folks understand that this is a working group, not a learning group or a book club. Undoubtedly things will be learned along the way, but that is not the main purpose of this group; this is a group of service. Don't take it personally if the person says no. Some people are ready, some are not. With every step of every process with this group, do not take things personally.

Some people have time constraints, some people don't feel ready, and some are just plain scared. Honor their decisions and let them know there are no hard feelings.

Set your first meeting date and let people who are interested know the time and place. This first meeting will be more of an exploratory time of folks being able to ask questions and clarify why they feel drawn to the group. After the first meeting, set the next meeting date (we meet every two weeks) and inform the participants that they need to let the facilitator know before the next meeting if they plan on being part of the group or if they are bowing out. If it is like most things, you may have to contact some of the participants who forgot to let you know or are on the fence about joining. By giving a deadline, you avoid drawing out the process.

Janice: During our brainstorming session of who to invite, we came up with a list of about 20 people. Most of them were people I knew, but several were also suggested by D and S. I sent out a blanket email to everyone explaining what we were doing and giving some background and information. Person-to-person would have been better, and that's why I'm suggesting that for you. Some people were very confused, but it seemed like a good idea at the time! At our first meeting we had 11 people that showed up at D and S's house. It was very casual and we all had a glass of wine to go with our meeting. (In retrospect, the wine was a bad idea and after several meetings, we instituted the policy of no drinking until after the meeting was over.) We placed chairs in a circle and each person took a turn explaining about why they were drawn to participate, what they saw as a focus for this group, and briefly what their spiritual journey was. (We went into spiritual journeys more in depth at later meetings.) This is the number that came to meetings for about the first six months.

Chapter 2:

HOW TO CONDUCT FIRST MEETINGS

The first few meetings are going to be focused on getting to know one another and creating a group energy and cohesiveness. Some sort of ritual for opening the meeting is good to mark a beginning to the meeting and to let everyone focus their attention on the group and leave behind whatever thoughts or personal issues they brought in with them. In the interest of sustaining the group energy, each person then takes a turn to briefly give an update on what is going on in their life and to share anything they wish about their spiritual journey that may have happened since the last meeting. Let people know this is not a time for rants about politics, environmental issues, or anything like that - or things that are too personal like their sex lives (*yes, one person did go there!*). The facilitator is the person that directs this. It should be emphasized from the beginning that there is no talking from anyone other than the person speaking. If there are questions or comments, they should be saved until that person has finished their update. From the beginning, emphasis should be given that any personal information shared within the group is to remain only in the group and not to be shared with those outside the group unless permission is given. If you find that people are talking too long or over-sharing, it is a good idea to bring some sort of timing device (Insight Timer phone app has a lovely chime) to let them know when time is up. If they are over-sharing, the facilitator should talk to them privately about what is appropriate to share.

Start and end your meetings on time; it needs to be expressed that folks should arrive on time if at all possible. Once the meeting has started, it is difficult to maintain the meditative and cohesive state if people are wandering in a few at a time. Life happens and sometimes people are going to be late. Let them know that, if possible, they should let another group member know they are coming but will be late, and when they enter, do so quietly and wait until whoever is speaking has stopped to enter the room and the circle. If someone is going to miss the meeting entirely, they should let the facilitator know so that the group won't be expecting them. If people are joining via Zoom or Skype, make sure the link is set up and ready to go a few minutes before the meeting begins. Ending the meeting on time assures that people can plan on a block of time to schedule around.

Janice: We decided that two hours was the right time frame to hold our meetings every other week on Sunday evening. We have changed the day and time several times to accommodate changing schedules, but we keep the two hour block of time. To begin the meeting, our group holds hands in a circle (left hand up to receive energy, right hand down to send energy) and I ask everyone to take a couple of deep breaths and bring their attention to the circle. When we began using Zoom for meetings after several members relocated, we just raise our hands to energetically connect to our circle. If any members are absent, their names are spoken and their energy is included in the circle. I ask them to let the energy flow between us in the circle, then let our breaths be with one breath, and our hearts beat with one beat. Then we open our eyes and come back into the present. I usually start with the person on my left for check-in time. We found that if you are interested and invested in the happiness and welfare of the other participants, the group dynamic is much more powerful. Over the years, we have had to pull back a few times on how much time people were taking and what kinds of things they were sharing. This happened a couple of times when we included new members who didn't know the protocol and we forgot to tell them.

As a way of group focus, it may be helpful to develop a mission statement. Talk about it, toss in ideas and concepts of what you want to accomplish as a group, and what you think needs to be accomplished for humanity, for the earth, for the universe. What-ever the group comes up with is the beginning of a direction. Note that this mission statement is not necessarily written in stone, it can be changed and updated as the group matures and finds focus.

Janice: This was our first mission statement - "We are diverse humans with similar experiences with soul planes of giving to somewhere and something. BUT, together we want to make a bigger contribution – there is a different level than just with our individual efforts. This is a soul heart love thing."

Take some time to let each person express what they think their strengths are and what they bring to the group. One person may be a channeler, one may be able to lead guided meditations, etc. If anyone does not know what they bring to the group, they can be assured that as time goes on their role will clarify. No one should be pressured into assuming a role they are uncomfortable with. Remember there is no reason to rush through any of this. A good foundation needs to be established if the group is to be able to sur-vive for the long haul.

Janice: To begin with, most people did not know their roles but many had strengths that they didn't think were important. One of our members had been an MP in the Army and she felt like her job was protection; another member had been in a meditation group for years and was able to channel; one member owned a yoga studio and had an expansive knowledge of chanting and the yoga sutras. One Jewish woman felt like her job was to carry the lineage of Jewish heritage. It seemed that each person was mostly willing to step up and do what they knew how to do.

In addition to letting people define their roles, another important step is to allow people to tell the story of their spiritual journey. This promotes understanding of where each one is coming from and where they see themselves headed. There will be similarities and there will be differences. By sharing this information, stronger bonds of trust are forged, and it may help the person see more clearly the role they will play in the group dynamics. Just like during check-in time, the person speaking should not be interrupted while they are telling their story; questions should be saved for when their narrative is completed.

Janice: For many of us, myself included, this process of telling one's spiritual journey felt like the innermost secrets of our souls were being exposed. Turns out we all felt like the black sheep of our families and friends since our beliefs were so radically different than most. After all the stories had been told (over the course of several meetings) there was a bond between us that had not been there before. We told who we really were and no one told us we were crazy. One of the other things we did in our first meetings was to select one participant at each meeting (we used a pendulum to decide who) to be the recipient of the group energy for that meeting. That person would then sit in the center of the circle, and for about 10 minutes, each person in the *circle would focus loving energy on that person. Just another way to let people bond and learn to trust each other. One of the early participants insisted that we have something tangible to focus on and we decided to each get a copy of **The Seat of the Soul** by Gary Zukav. For the first few meetings we would read a chapter and then spend about 10-15 minutes of the meeting time discussing the material. This soon fell by the wayside as we began to go into other things more pertinent to our mission.*

When the time period for the meeting has come to a close, it is good to bring it to a formal end. Have one person in the group do the closing, just as a person does the opening. This brings a finality to end the work you have undertaken at this meeting. It marks the end of the meeting and the beginning of time for personal visiting, pot luck dinner, or whatever you choose to do when the meeting is concluded, even if that is just going home.

Janice: I am usually the one, as the group facilitator, who does the opening, and I intuitively choose who will do the closing. My guidance is that everyone should have a turn at closing so they feel included and contributing to the group. There is no set way to close - some say whatever comes into their mind, some chant, some say a prayer. One of our members is Jewish and when it is her turn, she sings a closing prayer in Hebrew. Some are more willing than others to do the closing. There was one member who absolutely hated when I called on her to close because she was more of an introvert, but she had the most beautiful closings that came straight from her heart. Reiterate to members that there is no judgement about how they close the meeting, it is individual and exposes the group to a variety of life experiences and kinds of spirituality.

Chapter 3:

THE IMPORTANCE OF SOCIAL INTERACTION AND FOOD

What is this chapter doing here you might ask. After all, this isn't a social club or a night out with friends. This is a serious working group.

Yes and no are the answers. As I mentioned before, group cohesiveness is vital to keeping this group strong and active. As you work together for a longer period of time, the bond will develop and trust will deepen. However, just like the need for check-ins, it is important for the group to get to know each other - their personalities, their family dynamics, their interests, their hopes and fears, and their backgrounds.

There are several ways to do this. As many church organizations have figured out over the years, one of the best ways of gathering is with food. It is recommended that after the meeting that your group build in some time to have a meal together. That can be a pot luck at your meeting place, or at a nearby restaurant. Depending on the size of the group, it is often more convenient to just have everyone bring a dish and then there is no time needed to pack things up and head out to eat somewhere else. Or, you can create your own way of doing this. Please don't skip this step, it is important. People joining on Zoom or Skype can still participate in the same way as they did during the meeting. Just sit the laptop on the table and dine together.

Janice: With our group, someone suggested this at one of our first meetings and we all thought it was a good idea. As I mentioned previously, we soon opted to only have water or a non-alcoholic beverages during the meeting time, and then usually would have wine with our meal if desired. We made this a low stress process; there was no menu or no food sign-up sheet, you just brought what you wanted to bring. Amazingly we rarely had duplicate dishes and never ended up with all desserts. I remember these dinners with much fondness, it was a time we all got to know one another on a different level. There was a lot of laughter and a lot of sharing. Since we had a big group, it ended up being conversations with 2 or 3 people at a time, and we all tried to switch who we sat with in order to get to know everyone. Also, we had some really good food.

Another thing that is helpful is to have a semi-annual or annual retreat. This can be in the form of everyone gathering at one house, or a public venue like a park, or even taking a short road trip. An extended amount of time spent together can deepen the bonds shared between members and allow each person to reveal a little more about themselves. In two hour meetings it is sometimes hard to get a feel for who the other members are and what their lives are like. This is also a good time to set new goals and review what you have already been working on. Without periodic reflection things can get stale or members can feel like they are not contributing to their fullest, or are over-contributing.

Janice: While this is a good idea and one our group recommends, we don't always practice what we preach. Early on, the meals after the meetings served this purpose well, but when we had to change meeting times to accommodate schedules, we stopped having regular meals together and instead will go out to lunch after the meetings sometimes. Early on we took short road trips to Virginia Beach to go to the Association for Research and Enlightenment (A.R.E. - Edgar Cayce) and used their meditation room and garden and walked their amazing labyrinth. Most recently we scheduled a one day retreat at a local nature reserve where one member lives. We had pot luck food and some activities to do – some that were work, and some that were fun. We all also got chiggers from walking around in the woods. That is a group bonding experience if there ever was one!

It is encouraged to keep in touch, in person or by phone or email, with individual group members. These are people who are already on your wave length and it is good to support and develop friend-ships outside of the group. Of course this is up to each individual to do at their level of comfort. It is often the case that members may have similar interests, or are interested in what another member is doing. By making these deeper connections, teamwork is also being built. If there is knowledge and trust with another person on an individual level, trust is more easily given when energy work is being done.

Janice: When we started our group, I knew most of the members, but many did not know each other. For example, one of the women I barely knew talked about her horses, one big and two minis. I was enthralled at the prospect of being able to get up close and personal with some mini horses, so I asked if I could come out to the pasture and meet them. She had acquired them as a result of their former owner's neglect and they were scared of people. I committed to coming out once a week to do reiki with them and to help socialize them. During those weekly visits, C and I forged a deep and loving friendship that was, and is, mutually beneficial. (Plus I have some awesome horse friends now too!) We started a "secret" Facebook page where we share information about everything from what the energy is doing at the moment, sharing dreams and asking for interpretations, asking for advice about how to handle situations, if someone is ordering essential oils or crystals offering to get what group members need, book and movie recommendations, and many other various things that are well understood by the group, but not necessarily the general public. We also have text threads for the group that some people prefer to Facebook.

Chapter 4:

WHAT TO START WORKING ON

Here are a few suggestions about things to do at your meetings until you get up to speed with your own direction.

~Pick a place in the world where there is a natural disaster, conflict, or need of any kind and have a group meditation to send energy to that place and those people.

~Have a group meditation focusing on world peace.

~Focus on a group of endangered animals, plants, trees, or places and send energy toward their highest good.

~Spend some group meditation time focusing on sending healing and clarity for the oceans and fresh waters of the earth.

These are just a few things you can work on and it may spur you to consider other things. Suggested time for these meditations is 15-30 minutes in silence. A discussion can follow about what each person experiences during the meditation.

Remember, you are making your own rules. What I have written here are merely suggestions. When there is discussion and inner guidance among group members, new ideas can and will come up as a focus for your group. Any effort toward positive energy and higher vibration is a good thing, you can't do it wrong.

Janice: Our group was fortunate to have folks with particular skill sets that were very useful in helping us find direction. R had been part of a spiritual group for 20 years in New York, and through that learned channeling. I am a hypnotherapist and was accustomed to leading people into a meditative state (also I am sometimes bossy which makes me the perfect facilitator!), C has a real connection and communication with animals. R was able to channel information for the group about purpose and direction, which was very helpful. I suspect there will be people in your group that step forward with unique skills that are beneficial. Given time and encouragement, most every member of the group has found their "job". For some who can't seem to find their job, I feel personally like they may be there to hold space, provide grounding, and/or provide light and high vibration.

Chapter 5:

HOW TO MOVE FORWARD
WHEN PEOPLE DROP OUT

Inevitably there will be people who join the group that decide, for whatever reason, that they no longer want to be a group participant. Do not take this personally. From the beginning it should be made clear to every member of the group that if a time comes when they feel it is their time to leave, there will be no hard feelings and no judgement from anyone in the group. Each person's journey is honored and their journey may be with the group for a time, and then their path may take them in a different direction. It is no one's fault, it is just a fact of life. Some are only meant to be part of the group for a certain duration to contribute to the needs of the group at a particular time.

Janice: Our first dropouts came when we had planned a meeting to receive and ground some energy from the equinox. One of our members had a labyrinth in her yard, and we were to gather there. I had done a lot of study and planning to make this a special event for our group and was even a little nervous about leading this. Earlier in the day I got a text message that two of the women decided this was not the direction they were comfortable with and they were dropping out. Thirty minutes before the meeting, I got a message from two other people, the founders of the group, that they too were dropping out, citing family issues. I was completely devastated and took it very personally and did a lot of crying that night (we had not had the talk about people leaving). I thought I had done something wrong and that they were pushing me and/or the group away. It took a little time and talking to understand that this was a pivotal point in our group development. We were beginning our real work and this event was to separate those who were on this path and those that were not. No judgement. The four that left that day have gone on to do other amazing things that are more aligned with who they are.

As time has moved forward, we have had the majority of the group drop out for various reasons, and at one point were only a core group of three. We still moved forward and did some good work and became very close. Along the way others were considered to be added to the group; some chose not to join after talking with us, but some others did think it would be a good fit. It seemed that when we started a new focus for our work, people would come around that had particular skills that would be useful to our mission. So please understand that people leaving is not necessarily a bad thing, but rather a redefinition of group direction and dynamics.

What about sabbaticals? There will be times when a person is still wholeheartedly supportive of the group and the group mission, but will have life events that necessitate them taking some time off. There could be family illness, job pressures, or many other things that can affect the lives of group members. It is then up to the group to support the decision of that member to take some time off. They may have an idea when they will return, they may not. Some will not return at all. It is a good idea to periodically talk as

BRINGING IN THE LIGHT

a group about level of commitment to the group and the group mission. This may give some the opportunity to leave if they have been thinking about it, or to take some time off if they need it. It is up to your group to make the rules about this.

Janice: Over the years we have had several members who have taken sabbaticals. A couple of times we have suspended meetings for a month or six weeks in the summer when a lot of people were going to be gone or have visitors. The reasons for these sabbaticals have been varied. One member had a mother-in-law who lived with him who was in the last stages of her life. He took time off to help care for her and for his wife as she cared for her mother. One was having a personal crisis of faith and self awareness and needed time to re-center herself. One had a teaching job that was going to take her out of town most of the summer. One was going through a divorce. While they are gone, the group still includes their energy in our opening and still considers them part of the group dynamics whether they are there physically or not. They continue to be included until they tell us otherwise. It is sometimes tricky to know how to handle these situations when the person says they want to come back but when their reason is finished (like a death or end of other commitment) and they still are not returning. My personal way of dealing with it is to just let it work itself out. Mostly there will come some point when they will make the decision to leave permanently or will have a renewed sense of purpose and come back. Let me say again that when people decide to leave, don't take it personally. As sensitive individuals, which if you are in this kind of group you are, we tend to look for reasons why a person would choose to leave and perhaps our part in that. In all likelihood, their leaving has nothing to do with you or the group, but for their own reasons, even if they are reasons you don't understand.

Chapter 6:

LEARNING TO TRUST – MESSAGES AND EACH OTHER

As your group matures, one or more of you may get messages for the group. This could come in a meditative state, through dreams, through a channel, or some other way. Often several members of the group will get the same or similar messages. Encouragement should be given to share these messages after the check-ins are complete. Like pieces of a puzzle, each person may be given a bit of information that doesn't make sense until combined with information that others in the group have received. Don't be shy about sharing the messages you receive in the group; it is likely there are others who have received messages that may be reluctant to share, especially when the group is new or there are new members.

How do you know to trust these messages? This is something most people and most groups struggle with, at least at first. There is no definitive way to say that you should trust or not trust. Generally speaking, if it is coming from a place of love and peacefulness, you can trust it. If it comes across as destructive, dark, or sarcastic, it is a cause for concern whether this is a trustworthy source. Ultimately you, and the group, must decide if this is trustworthy information.

This is another reason why group cohesion and communication outside of the meeting are vital. If you know another person on more levels than just the time you spend with them in the setting of a meeting, you are more prepared to know whether their information feels trustworthy. If it does not, find a kind way to question it and ask the group to perhaps table the action associated with the information until the next meeting. At that time, perhaps talk to the facilitator and let them know you are uncomfortable with it. It is then up to the facilitator to steer the meeting away from that subject at future meetings.

Janice: Our group finds it helps if each person has a way that they communicate with spirit. Some meditate, some handle crystals, some channel, some dream. In our early meetings, we relied on our one person that was a long time channeler for most of our direction. As we all got more comfortable with our own way of getting information, we began to more freely share. Personally, I used to question my information frequently. It was as if I didn't think I was worthy enough to be given this level of knowledge. Gradually I began to trust myself and more sources more completely, but at the beginning I would use my pendulum for a yes/no response of whether I should trust this information.

In later years, as we have all become more sure of ourselves, we find it helpful to share what we have received and are usually delighted to put together the puzzle that has been given to us. As we have gone deeper and deeper into our work, we find that this almost always happens. I am no longer surprised when I receive what seems like a nonsensical message, almost always it makes sense when combined with what others receive.

I do want to take a moment to caution you about messages that don't feel right. There was a person who was not in our group, but was a regular channeler who would tell me things he was receiving and felt absolutely sure of himself. I found his messages to be dark and foreboding, and often about cataclysmic events that were coming. At first, I felt that I had no right to question his information, but the vibration of his messages never resonated with me. Always trust yourself if it doesn't resonate with your own vibration. You will know.

Another thing that will most likely take place is intuitive "hits" about places to go and/or things to do. Take a moment to notice if a hit feels right or not. You can discuss these within the group or act on them individually. For example, you may be drawn to go to a particular place in nature like the woods or a beach. When you get there the purpose for your visit becomes clear. It may be to receive energy, to discover an object that was left there for you, or any number of things. The point is, if you feel strongly about something, then you should do it and not worry about whether you will look or feel foolish. As you begin to open more and more, you will begin to trust yourself and your group more completely. Remember, lightwork is not for the faint of heart! You will be pushed out of your comfort zone over and over until your comfort zone encompasses things you would have never imagined.

Janice: In 2011, I felt strongly called to go to California to Sequoia National Park to do some energy clearing with the giant redwoods. I was living in North Carolina at the time, so this was a big trip to make just going on my intuition. I had been to Sequoia before and felt the big trees held such ancient wisdom. In a meditation, I was told that these trees had been collecting negative energy so humans would not be affected, but they were at capacity after holding it for thousands of years. We were heading into the shift of 2012 and it felt imperative that some energy work be done with these trees. I had no idea what that really meant or how to do it. But the message was strong enough that I acted on it. I did some research on energy clearing, got some flower essences from Perelandra, Ltd., got on a plane and went to California. My group fully supported me on this journey and I did daily check-ins with them. I did the work and was rewarded with little signs along the way. While I was there, I was also called on to visit Mt. Shasta and do some clearing there, as well as in a nearby veteran's park which was also near the place where there was a Japanese internment camp. All of these additional places were just intuitive and random (or not so random) people I didn't know along the way pointed me in the direction I needed to go. When you are open to synchronicity and guidance, you will always find the way.

Another group member did a meditation on his vacation in the desert and was shown in his mind's eye how to receive, ground, and distribute blue star energy, which we were working with at the time, also prior to 2012. At the end of his meditation, he felt skeptical about the information he received, and just then a small lizard climbed up his arm and stared at him about 2" from his face for a full minute and then left. The group used this method with much success.

You don't need to know how to do any of these specialties, you just need to trust that you will be given the information and guided in the correct direction. If the information or direction feels dark/low vibration, or off in any way, use your discernment about whether this is coming from a place of light and love. If you don't feel like it is, don't do it.

Chapter 7:

HOW AND WHEN TO ADD NEW MEMBERS

There will come a time when your group may have lost members for various reasons and the group energy no longer feels complete. There is no fixed correct number of participants, just trust (there is that trust thing again!) that you will know when it's time. It may evolve organically when one or more members runs across someone who they believe would be an asset to the group or has a particular skill set that is missing. It may be a group decision to actively begin looking for folks of like mind that are open to joining a lightworkers group. Be sure it is someone one of the group members know and have talked to the person about their beliefs and feelings about a group like this.

When the group has discussed the new person or persons, it is time to invite them to an informal meeting, such as lunch or even just the beginning of one of your regular meetings. This is the opportunity for the person to be given an overview of your work and for both sides to ask questions of the other. A list of questions should be discussed and listed in advance of this meeting. It is good to stick to the list to make sure all of the group's concerns are addressed. Some personal questions are fine to be included since it would be less than desirable to invite someone who has ongoing drama of one form or another. Examples of some questions to ask:

~How has your own spiritual journey led you to this place today?

~Do you have a regular practice of meditation or some other way of connecting with universal energy?

~What do you feel like you can contribute to this group?

~The specifics about individuals in this group are confidential, do you think you will be able to keep that confidentiality?

~We often go very deeply into meditative states and altered consciousness (like a hypnotic state) to do our work. Will you be all right and feel safe with that?

~We are committed to meetings every two weeks (or whatever your meeting schedule is) and ask that members make this group a priority. Will you be able to regularly come to meetings?

~Is there anything in your personal life that will or has the potential to interfere with your work in this group? (Examples may be child care, unsupportive spouse or partner, job/work.)

After your questions are asked and answered, give them an opportunity to ask questions. Be honest with your answers; if you skirt around issues you think they may not be comfortable with, the partnership will not work in the long run. Also notice how the energy of the group is with this person or persons present. Does the energy feel smooth and cohesive or does it feel incompatible or off? Pay attention to the unseen and unspoken as much as the seen and spoken.

After the interview, the group needs to take plenty of time to discuss the answers that were given and the energy that was felt. If there are any additional questions that come up, a phone call from the person who is the contact should suffice to obtain the answer. If any one person in the group has misgivings or doubts about the new member, then an offer should not be extended. Explain to the potential person that the group doesn't feel it will be a good fit, you don't owe them any longer explanation. If they press you for more, explain that the group discussion is confidential and you can't explain further. If, on the other hand, the group is in accord about inviting this person to join, then the contact person shall extend a formal invitation to join. There may be times when the invitation is extended and the invitee declines. They do not owe you any explanation other than they decline. Sometimes it is just not a good fit for one side of another.

If the new person accepts the invitation, let them know the next meeting date and time. If you are still doing potluck or some sort of post-meeting gathering, let them know about it so they come prepared. The first meeting with the new person or persons needs to be one of welcome and a more in depth explanation of what the group has been working on. Rules about check-in and conduct will be discussed and perhaps just general updates in each person's life in the group so the new person or persons will have more of an idea of who the people are that they are now in association with. Any kind of journey or "heavy" work should be avoided at their first meeting. It may take 2 or 3 meetings for them to feel fully integrated.

Be prepared that the group dynamics will change with each new person that arrives. This is especially true if the group has gone for a long time with no new members. It may feel strange or awkward for a while. This is a good time for the facilitator to check in with each group member individually (including the new person) to find out if things are sitting well with them after the new addition, and to smooth out any wrinkles that may be occurring.

Janice: Our group went four years before we added any new people. Our group size had shrunk to just four and we went for about a year with only four. At one point about year three, we identified a woman we thought would be a good addition, did a lunch date interview with her, and basically, she went screaming in the other direction, metaphorically speaking! She felt we were too "far out" for her and wasn't comfortable with what we were doing. So it happens that everyone doesn't think we are as wonderful as we think we are. Don't take it personally. After the fourth year with only four members, I identified two women who brought in not only strong and lovely energy, but a skill set with stones and crystals that we did not have and needed. They happily incorporated into the group. About two years later, three more women came in, one of whom is incredibly psychic. Then three left, and one more came in early in 2017. Only two of the original members remain at this writing, I am one of them. The dynamics of the group have changed but I feel with each new addition we strengthen and are guided in the direction we need to follow. So now I have to go back to not taking things personally. I was very sad when the last two of the four original members left just a few months ago. Yes, I cried about it and felt like they were ripping out a piece of my heart. Ultimately though, they had their own reasons for leaving and I had to let them go with love and gratitude. Just as a footnote, both of those members have now returned to the group. Not everyone is meant to be part of it forever. Each person brings the energy needed by the group at the time it is needed.

Chapter 8:

LEARNING TOGETHER

It is not likely that all group members will come in with a full skill set. Many will have been on their personal spiritual path, some for a number of years. Some will just have raw talent or enthusiastic energy.

There will be times, especially between projects, when you will have some down time. This is good and necessary for team building and learning. If you are constantly doing heavy energy work with no breaks, everyone in the group will get burned out. Accept these down times for what they are: rest before the next work detail. The group can identify what things may be helpful to know for accomplishing this work. Some group members will have these skills, some skills will have to be learned by everyone.

Once you have a list of what you need to learn, it's time to divide up the list and make assignments for people to investigate and present to the group. For some, it will be easy if they already have the skill set. For example, if someone has been doing work with crystals, or with channeling, for a long time, they are the natural choice to be the teachers of those skills. Allow people to volunteer what they would like to teach, and if no one volunteers, the facilitator should make assignments. It normally will not come to that; people are in the group because they want to make a difference and are willing to step up.

During these rest times, it will be up to the facilitator to schedule who will be presenting at the meetings. If the list is prioritized, just go down the list to the next thing. If the list is not prioritized, the facilitator should use their intuition to decide what skill needs to be learned next. It is a good idea for the facilitator to check in individually with people to see how they are coming with their lesson plans and identify if they are having difficulty with the subject matter. Encourage group members to communicate with each other for help and information during times between meetings.

If the person presenting has a need for people to bring specific things to the meeting, he or she should contact the group directly to share that information. For example, sometimes it is helpful for people to bring writing materials to make notes or record results. Sometimes the person teaching will provide materials for the group, such as printed material or references, or even physical things like crystals. Time should be given during the presentation for the group to practice what is being taught.

Janice: There is a fine line with this. Early in our group life, some people were present mostly because they wanted to learn and not to serve. It is when we began our work that many of those people dropped out. That is why it is important at the beginning to make sure people understand this is a working group, not a learning group.

That being said, there will naturally be learning that has to occur. Fifteen years into it, and I am still a student when I need to be. If anyone thinks they know everything, beware! This also serves as a relief for persons who may come in with a bigger skill set than others, you don't want them to get bogged down and feel like they are doing everything. I had to balance this with one of our members who had been channeling for about 20 years. We all trusted him to be a clear channel, but it also was not fair to him to be the only one doing that. So, he taught us how and we all now have some level of that ability, some more comfortable than others with this skill. It's all about practice. We had one woman who was particularly knowledgeable about stones and crystals, and she taught us what different stones are suitable for.. Another woman has an amazing connection to animals, and she is our go-to person for animal energy.

Everyone has something to contribute, even if it is just adding their energy to the group energy. Long ago (not in this group) I did work with a man who would go into such a deep meditative state when we were working that we thought he was going to sleep. Turns out that he was our energy and place holder when we were out gallivanting around the galaxy. It was imperative that we had a grounding presence since, at that time, we really had no idea what we were doing. The point of this story is that sometimes people will feel like they don't have a special skill to share or aren't contributing. My assertion is that this is not true, that everyone brings something to the table even if that something is not readily apparent.

Part Two:

THE HOW-TO GUIDE

Chapter 9:

TOOLS OF THE TRADE

This chapter will get into some specific ways to do things that are basic to, I believe, any lightworkers group. These are merely tried and true suggestions. If you or your group has a better way, then do it your way.

Hypnosis/meditative state/journeys

I'm starting with this because it seems that this is the backbone for many of the other tools. I suspect that if people are drawn to this group, they will already have a meditative practice, but it is good to step it up and go deeper.

A simple way to achieve a deep state is just to pay attention to the breath. Notice everything about it - how it feels when your chest rises and falls, how the temperature is different inhaling and exhaling, how your heartbeat slows, etc. If your attention strays, just bring yourself back to the breath.

To deepen the breath practice, and to promote self awareness, I have developed a technique called Spirit Breath Flow, which I cobbled together from several breath practices I learned over the years and from using hypnotic techniques. The beginning premise is that we are not only our bodies, but also are encased in our own energy field surrounding the body. Here's how it works: begin by breathing slowly and mindfully, letting your awareness be with the breath until the body feels calm. The next step is finding your body core, or center, is the first step. Primarily this is found in the area of the heart or solar plexus. Practice breathing through that center. One energy location at a time is then accessed using the breath - front, back, left side, right side, above and below. Using a deeper breath, draw in the energy from each area and let it rest in your center for a few breaths. During that time, allow any images, thoughts, feelings, or sensations to come into your mind, and then breathe them back out. Generally, the areas of energy correspond to parts of your life: Front - future; Back - past; Left side - feminine; Right side - masculine; Above - connection to Source; Below - connection to Earth. If it feels otherwise to you, trust your own intuition. There is no wrong way to do this practice.

Once everyone feels comfortable with their meditative practice, then I would suggest a group meditation led by whichever group member feels most confident. As mentioned in earlier chapters, this can be sending group energy to a part of the world that has a natural disaster going on, to a particular person or group that is in need of energetic assistance (sickness, grief, etc.), an animal group such as whales or an endangered species, or just to promote world peace in general. The next step is going on a group journey.

In a group hypnosis session, which is basically what a group journey is, if more than one person is going to a past life, one person agrees to be the leader and the other person or persons agree to be the followers. This can be a powerful bonding experience for the group to see where you may have worked together before. One person is designated to guide the leader into a relaxed or hypnotic state (other group members will also follow the relaxation until it is time to choose a place), and then ask that person to go back to a time when the group was together in the past and settle into that lifetime. The leader will begin to describe where they are and what is going on. The rest of the group is then invited to join them there. The guide may or may not be willing or able to participate. The leader will then take over and the group will add in experiences as they have them. Brian Weiss has a very good regression script at the end of his book Through Time Into Healing that can be used for this purpose.

Janice: This is a transcript of one of the journeys we took. We record them and then someone in the group will transcribe it. There were only three present at this meeting. R was the leader. Keep in mind that he has been doing this for years, your group leader may not experience the same level of imagery or depth.

April 17, 2011

R: I'm beaconing for you two to join me. There is water flowing under the bridge and a boat sitting on the bank on the side that we just crossed over to. We are to get into the boat and go down the river and let the river carry us. We step into the boat and keep it balanced as we board. We look back over on the other side of the bridge and R and B (group members not present) are standing there and they can't join us this time. So we wave goodbye to them and disembark. We're just floating down this lovely stream in this boat, just floating along, no oars or paddles, a small boat just right for 3 of us. Going downstream carried by the current. We're moving swiftly through the forest, through open fields, cows, horses, watching us pass, staying in the center of the stream. Moving through a dry terrain, a desert area, leaving all the green behind. Moving more into a desert terrain. Our stream has become a canal, a man-made canal. Date palms growing on the sides, children playing in the water, other boat traffic on the water. Men in boats with their nets, fish, children swimming, people drawing water out of the canal and we're moving more slowly now. We're dressed in white linens. Everyone is brown with black hair and children's white teeth are gleaming in the sunlight as they laugh and play in the water. Our boat edges up to some stairs that descend down to the water, great stone steps where many people are drawing water, women with urns. Our boat stops there at the stairs that descend to the water – they are used by everyone. They watch us as we step out of the boat into the water and onto the stone steps. We help each other step forward and climb to the top of the stairs and we're in a city in Egypt. The city is Alexandria on the coast of Egypt in the days of the library of Alexandria when it was at its height. It's a thriving city, people throng the streets. We're in our linens, everyone is dressed in white and cotton. We stop in the bazaar and see everything that's being sold – many different kinds of fish, dates, plums, peaches, pears, many fruits and grains, lentils and beans, great urns filled with everything, meats, salt, cured and fresh fish. Everyone buying and selling, great good feelings in the air, wonderful fragrances, spices and myrrh. Plants for sale. A vendor selling flowers. Colored patterns and fabrics for sale, the great din, we relish it, we're familiar with it and we celebrate this world. This is a long time ago. We are making our way to the library of Alexandria, the 3 of us. We are in search of specific information. We live in the city and we study in Alexandria in the library. Scholars. Here is the temple, that is what we call the library. What we do there is more like worship than studying. It is immense, pharaoh has not spared any expense in providing for the library. It grows each year to hold the thousands of scrolls that are housed here. Works by Plato and Socrates, all the great poets and playwrights of antiquity have their scrolls stored

BRINGING IN THE LIGHT

here. The librarians are honored by everyone in Alexandria as great and learned people. They protect and collect and archive everything and they search far and wide. We come to search a distant corner of this library. The librarian greets us, familiar with our faces. We feel the cool stone under our feet, the great pillars hold up the immense roof. Our guide walks us back to the set of scrolls we study. This is our life, studying these scrolls. We go to this place far from any other place in the library, quiet. Outside our window is a fountain and we hear the water and we quietly reach for our scrolls and unroll them. We read aloud to each other what we discover if it is something of interest to us. The scrolls are ancient texts that deal with the religion of Mithras. That's who and what we are studying. We are studying Mithras to compare the philosophy of that particular religion which is widespread to the information reaching us about religions of the peoples in Liberia and Gaul and those strange islands off the coast of Europe, filled with powerful beings that practice great magic in connection with the natural world. We are curious to understand how that knowledge relates to the Mithratic religion. Mithras, born of a virgin, wise men visited, the son of God. Mithras with a message of compassion began to inform and pave the way for another religion which was to come, each religion to build a path for the next to come after it, each religion a stepping stone. This is the information we share and understand. Each religion a stepping stone to the next as humanity evolves and opens its collective heart to understanding itself as part of the whole. At the moment we are studying ancient religions of the Middle East, especially the Mithratic religion and its relationship to its predecessor the pagan religions of Liberia and Gaul and the islands to the north. We study, we compare, we write. This is our life and for this we are compensated by the pharaoh and his priests consult with us on an ongoing basis. We are religious scholars together studying in the great library in Alexandria.

J; I feel like the pharaoh doesn't always like what we have to say about this and sometimes we have our asses chewed. Base our findings more on what the pharaoh wants to hear and not what we perceive as the truth.

R: Yes

J: But we 3 talk openly among ourselves about it. And there is a component written in this about visitors from other planets that is part of this. And that's the part the pharaoh doesn't like because the pharaoh wants to be the omnipotent. He doesn't want the others to be aware of the "others".

C: I am talking with you about a building, a temple, for this and it's secretive. I want to give you all the information pertaining to build the temple and the secret space we'll use.

J: We decide to go under a pyramid for the temple. There has been a great source of energy that has been put there by one of these other civilizations and I'm seeing an inversion of the pyramid and the power source at the apex (top/bottom) under the earth. We know it's there because we've read and studied the scrolls and talked to the "others" but the others are afraid this will be misused by the pharaoh so we can't tell. But we're being given instructions on how to find our way to this power source, as if they left a pathway for us. But only through studying these scrolls do we have the information to get to it and that's where we want to build the temple. The temple won't be for everyone, at least not yet. What else are you feeling about this?

C: One of you is my brother

J: It's R

C: And I feel like we're all brothers. The design is possible, this can be done. The librarian knows and that's why we can ......(can't hear the rest). We can trust the librarian.

J: There's deeper purpose to this but I can't put my finger on what it is.

R: Now we're understanding from our studying that religions of northern Europe and western Europe contain important remnants from Atlantean culture and we're connecting the lessons of Atlantis to what is unfolding the in the Mediterranean culture.

J: We remember the lessons for Atlantis and we're trying not to repeat them.

R: Yes

J: And with this pharaoh we're coming dangerously close to repeating. And there's a connection between the energy source and the one we're studying - Mithras.

R: Yes

J: The librarian knows.

R: The librarian speaks in whispers to us about these matters. The information learned here was vital to the information we developed and extended when we were living in Angor Wat. That is where much of our knowledge was first learned.

J: And each time we remember, just like we're doing now. I feel like the 3 brothers have a message for us, but I don't know what it is.

R: One part of the message is to rediscover and restudy the Mithratic religion, to study Mithras and the philosophy, particularly its mystical elements, and incorporate it's central teachings with the Atlantean culture. Before the Atlantean culture began to spiral downward, and the others know that energy source is still there,

J: It is;

R: Understand you thinking about it.

J: It holds information and what we have to do is connect with that source and it will be as if we are back in the Alexandria library and everything is there that we need to know.

C: That scroll that has the information is not in the library. The librarian has told us that there are scrolls that are missing.

J: So we need to get that information and study it.

R: We must now stand from our table in the library and leave. The sun is setting. We can hear the fountain and the water and birds chirping, and so quietly we roll our scrolls up and the librarian takes them to put in their proper place. We walk out of the library together. Because of our dress and our jewelry, people know that we are emissaries of the pharaoh. We pass through the streets and through the bazaar as the sun sets, and see vendors putting their wares away, folding their awnings. Dust is everywhere, children are running; we approach the canal and our boat slides in to meet us. We descend the stone stairs and find our seats in the boat. We pull away from the stairs and begin to move up the canal away from the city in Alexandria, away from the din in the city. The sun sets and we move with the current gradually through the desert and then into the trees and the dense forest, green *and cool. Before us we see the bridge and our boat comes to the side and we disembark. We are no longer brown and dark haired and no longer speaking an ancient language and reading hieroglyphics and ancient Greek. We step onto the bridge and before we move to the middle of the bridge, we pause in case any of us has an additional thing to say or has insights about our journey.*

J: The only thing that comes to my mind is the word remember – just remember.

R: It is with the deepest of understandings that we cross the bridge where R and B are waiting for us and we walk together down a path to return.

Not only was this a bonding experience for the group, but closer to the December, 2012 energy shift, our group was called on to activate pyramids all over the earth. I remembered this journey and how the pyramid had an inverted apex and we discovered through a channel that there was a large crystal there that needed to be activated. We did this activation through another group journey where we went to the crystal and all placed hands on it with the intention of activation and found it coming alive under our hands. This was the blueprint we used for other pyramids we were called to work with.

Once we figured out we needed to work with pyramids, the synchronicity of finding them was astounding. We would see a news article, or a science show, or other different ways, about pyramids that had been discovered or hidden. It was no coincidence these came into our awareness just at the right time when we were called to do this work.

Channeling

Channeling is one of those areas that people are usually either comfortable with or not, few are in between. Some may feel that they are not worthy to talk to those in other dimensions, or that they will get the message wrong. There will be those in your group who are more suited than others and they will be identified fairly soon after your group begins its work. Your group can, of course, elect not to use channeling, but in one form or another your group will rely on them. They can be as simple as just intuition, or a knowing, or it can be talking to another entity or group. I will include in the next part a set of instructions called The Discursive Meditation, discursive meaning interactive between you and whomever you are channeling. If you have a different method that works for you, by all means use it. This is offered as a starting point for opening up to channeling.

It is wise to envision yourself surrounded in light (*white, gold, blue, or green are what I find best*) as you are beginning. Lower vibrational energies are also most willing to be channeled but that is not your target entity. As the instructions state, find who represents a higher vibration or divine guidance for you and make that the intention of your channel. As you are more practiced, you will find that you can channel not only divine or other dimensional energies, but also anything with living energy, which is basically everything. It may be helpful to practice this by yourself for a while, perhaps by writing as you channel, or speaking into a recorder.

Automatic writing is a good beginning way to channel. Sit down with a pen and paper, or in front of the computer, and just take a few breaths and begin writing. It doesn't matter if it starts out being nonsensical, just keep writing whatever comes into your head with the intention that it be from your higher self or a high vibration energy, but higher self is a good one to start with. If you practice this, soon you will begin to feel the difference in your energy when you are "you" and when you are channeling someone else.

Especially early on, remember that you are raising your level of energy and they are lowering theirs to meet you. What this means for you physically and emotionally is that at the end of the channel you may find yourself to be very tired and/or very emotional. This is normal and there is no reason for alarm. Just rest and be gentle with yourself.

When you are doing a speaking channel, and sometimes with a written one, be prepared to receive pictures in your mind's eye to go along with what you are saying or writing. This is a method they use to convey additional information to you so you will understand the message more clearly. It is not necessary to describe these images to anyone else unless you think it will enhance what is being transmitted. Channeled entities use whatever knowledge and skills you already have to make the message understandable to you, and this includes the use of image. For example, if you didn't know Spanish, your channel would not be in that language; or if your education was not in engineering, changes are your information would not be in technical terms. If you are not sure who you are channeling, ask. They will be glad to share that information. See the section on animals for more information about communicating with them.

Above all, trust yourself. There will be times you feel like you are just making things up. That is natural and normal. As you practice more you will be able to discern what is your mind chatter and what is channeled information.

Janice: My first attempts at channeling were exactly what I have suggested. I took a class that included automatic writing and felt very silly writing things like "I'm sitting here writing something because I'm supposed to be writing something. The sky is blue, the sun is warm." But it never failed that by just continuing to write, I often came out with some beautiful words. Nothing earth shattering or profoundly wise, but a nice message. As I got more comfortable with that, I started the session with some deep breathing and then the writing lost its nonsensical quality and gradually became deeper and more meaningful.

Then one day in yoga class (I was the only one that showed up that day) I felt an overwhelming urge to speak for someone (it was my higher self). The yoga instructor was one of the group members at the time so she understood. I channeled spoken word for about 10 minutes. When I was finished, I burst into tears and did the ugly cry. The first 10 or so times I did spoken channel this happened to me, and then I realized that it was the difference in energy and vibration I was feeling. It was as if I was flying high and communing with the saints, and all of a sudden, I was dropped like a rock back into the lower vibration of being a human. As my vibration has raised, this no longer happens.

I first began channeling my higher self, and as I said, I got messages mostly for myself. Later, as I began spoken channel, I asked and was told that I was channeling "The Council", which are 12 members of the Elohim, or wise ones, that offer advice to humans who are doing light work, or work to raise the vibration of the Earth and her inhabitants. As my skills have progressed, I am now able to channel not only The Council and my higher self, but also animals, minerals, etc. Since all things have their own energy, if you can tune into the vibration and simply ask, you can talk to them.

BRINGING IN THE LIGHT

The following Discursive Meditation instructions are what my group has used in the past to help members begin getting comfortable with channel. At a few meetings we did this process as a group and then were silent during the Response phase. In a safe setting within the group, some amazing messages were shared. This comes back to group dynamics creating a safe space to explore with encouragement and without judgement.

This is from our member R, who was in a spiritual/meditation group for 20+ years and learned how to use and teach this technique.

The Discursive Meditation

This particular meditational technique is designed to offer a way to deepen and develop one's spiritual experience. It allows a person to communicate with (channel) the most encompassing universal intelligence, thereby allowing you to receive guidance, reassurance, and inner peace.

If one wishes, it can be practiced several times a day. Initially, however, it is recommended that you meditate once a day, in the morning, before doing anything else, at the same time each day. Also, at the beginning, it's fine to set aside a relatively short period for meditating (9 or 15 minutes), and work up to a half hour. If you create the time and have the inclination, you can meditate both in the morning and in the evening.

To prepare to meditate, find a quiet space and sit in a chair with feet together, hands together (in "open prayer" fashion), with your back straight and shoulders relaxed. The idea is to be in a comfortable position, with your body's energies able to circulate, so that you can meditate without distractions. Before meditating, give yourself a little time to relax, recollect yourself, breathe calmly, and to let go of any concerns, worries, plans and the like. Make this your time to build inner strength/resilience, spiritual health, and a relationship with the wider universe.

The meditation consists of three steps - the Invocation, the Silence and the Response. Each step should last for either 3 minutes, or 5 minutes, or 10 minutes, resulting in a meditation that lasts for 9 minutes, 15 minutes or half an hour. You'll need a watch or clock that you can consult during the meditation from time to time so that you can stay on track, temporally-speaking. Your eyes should be closed (except when peeking at the time-piece).

During the Invocation, you further calm yourself, center your attention, invoke God (or the Divine Mother, or Lord Brahma, or Holy Presence, or Great Universe, or whatever you wish to call the most inclusive Thing you can imagine to exist), and introduce the topic of your meditation - which can be a question, a concern, a call for assistance, an opportunity to expand - whatever you wish. Repeat the following words three times, with increasing slowness, and in rising pitch with each repetition: "Discursive Meditation." Then say, "Invocation...Divine Mother [or whatever term you wish to use], I invoke you with my heart...I invoke your presence with my heart... please help me to... [And here you ask for help with whatever you need or are seeking: insight, joy, consolation, direction, bliss, making a choice, etc.]. You can repeat this part of the meditation several times. After a third of the time of the entire meditation (three, five or ten minutes) has passed, then stop and say, "Silence."

During the Silence, you simply wait in stillness and calm, thinking about nothing, if possible. Let all the thoughts and concerns that normally "grab" your attention calmly go by. Don't engage with them. This is usually difficult, especially at first. So it is okay to concentrate on a simple, calming image during the Silence phase - an image of *a burning candle, a snow-covered mountain, a sleeping baby, your breathing, the Earth in space, the heart-beat of humanity... Stay in Silence for a third of the time of your meditation.*

In the Response period, you simply let the voice of the Divine speak through you. You let go completely and simply let the Universe flow through you with its insights, love, guidance, images, etc. Sometimes there are no words – simply images, or a fragrance, or an even deeper, more profound sense of inner peace. And that's fine. But most often there are words, and you simply allow them to come through while remaining very relaxed and paying attention. At the end of the allotted time, allow the Response to come to a close, and say "Peace." That will bring your meditation to a close. Afterwards, you can write down what you remember of the Response, if you wish.

I often find it helpful to simply sit quietly for a few moments after practicing the discursive meditation to allow myself time to readjust to the world, its demands, etc. You might notice that it is often the case that a kind of peace will remain with you through the day, bringing a calm, a more loving ability to interact with others (and yourself!), greater efficiency and clarity of mind, and other things. It affects everyone a bit differently.

The entire meditation can be done in silence, or said out loud. For those beginning this meditation, saying the words aloud sometimes helps you to concentrate. With time and practice, however, the meditation seems to become more naturally internal, and can be done in complete silence. One sometimes seems to get a bit "more mileage" out of the meditation when it practiced in silence, but that depends on the person.

Animals as guides and helpers

The animal kingdom is so much more connected to the earth than humans are. Chances are one or more people in your group will have a real affinity and connection with animals, whether domestic or wild. An internet search will reveal spiritual meanings of different animals. Depending on the mission of your group, many times members will begin seeing similar animals. When looking up the meanings, the animal can provide assistance to the group in the form of direction or advice. Steven Farmer has several good books - Animal Spirit Guides and Power Animals are two very good ones that give explanations. There are even phone apps for some of these for quick information when you're out and about.

The way to communicate with animals (and plants and minerals) is a bit different. In that world, there is what is called a deva that represents the group energy. Sometimes you will get an individual animal, but most often you will be talking to the deva of that species. There is an excellent description of what is called a "coning", which is like a conference call between a human and a devic entity. Machelle Small Wright has an excellent description on her website www.perelandra-ltd.com and in several of her books. A small caveat - she refers to the White Brotherhood in this coning technique. Before you think it's a group of Ku Klux Klan members, White Brotherhood refers to a group of ascended masters that are there to help humanity.

Animals can provide great assistance and insight to lightworker groups. They have ancient wisdom that is unsullied by human emotion and perspective. Trees, in particular among the plant community, also possess this ancient wisdom - especially the oldest species like sequoias. The coning techniques work with plants and minerals as well as animals.

Janice: About 1-1/2 years into our group experience, we began to talk about animals as guides. R began channeling animal devas in his 20's when he started gardening. He had gophers who kept eating all of his plants and he was growing very frustrated. So he asked to speak to the gopher deva, whom he described as very grumpy. They came to an arrangement that R would literally draw a line in the sand (dirt) and the gophers could eat everything on their side of the line, but were to leave the plants on his side of the line alone. Much to R's delight, it worked.

Our member C, who has an amazing animal connection, led us on a journey to discover our own animal guides (her instructions are below) and at the end of the journey, she asked that we be told who our animal guide was for the group. Great blue heron showed up for us. We all lived in a coastal area at that time, so these graceful birds were common. However, even as common as they were, they would show up for all of the group members at times when we were med-itating, or had some other sort of "woo-woo" experience. At one of our meetings shortly after, our member R channeled the great blue heron deva for us. The channel follows the instructions to give you an example.

Great Blue Heron Deva Channel

June 13, 2010   *channeled by R*

Coastal Indians have been invoking the spirit devas hundreds of years ago – humans have known heron deva for a long time. (There was some reference to them using heron for dance.)

I come gently but uneasily amongst you – I don't know you well but you are kindred so I come to you. I am here, I listen to reverberations of your conversation earlier and I understand your sentiment. Know that there is great sadness about the tragedy in the animal world we call this oil spill the tragedy (this is in reference to the Gulf of Mexico oil spill). It cannot be ignored or a different kind of wrath will come upon you. Other groups have chosen me as a totem – I am moving between different groups of beings, that unites the thoughts of different coastal creatures. I agree to serve as your totem, for a service it is. I will come to your meetings, I can be this emissary for you, will voice your thoughts to the world.

I will ask that you continue to deepen yourselves. As one of you voiced earlier, you are still in the bottom rungs of the ladder. You are awakened but you can awaken more. Climb until you have the full view, until the only thing you have left in your hearts is reverence and love.

Know that one of the reasons you have chosen me if you are conscious or not, I have laser attention. When I hunt, that is all I do; when I fly, that is all I do; when I raise my young, that is all I do. The lesson for you, focus with laser intensity on the growth of the group. Giving of gifts, spiritual gifts to the wider world – some of you are doing this.

Look with me now with my own eyes while I walk upon the shores of a healthy marsh. The vision is far wider, peering into the water, see reflections of light – the ripples, by the mud, by my feet, each movement of the blade of grass – in a way human beings can't fathom. Fish come into view, I strike with my beak. I maneuver it quickly to my mouth, into my being, down my throat. The energy of the fish is transferred into heron. I live directly in the moment seeking only to live well.

Come back into your senses, into bodily human form. I invited you to heron awareness for a moment to experience the vast difference. Humans are experiencing a great shift in consciousness. We welcome that.

I place my wings around you now. Feel them encircle the group, enfold you. Do you have any questions?

J: Why do we need a guide from the animal kingdom, what is the purpose in this?

Heron: I bow to you, such an interesting question. The last group that so depended on me and contacted me were Native Americans hundreds and thousands of years ago. They knew they depended on the presence of me and the other devas. I am the balance. I represent non-human balance and perspective, you need that.

J: Is there anything we can do in our group to make a difference in the tragedy?

H: What would you have me convey to the other devas? This will help, along with your work, it is felt everywhere.

J: Our message to devas: We hold you dear to our hearts, we endeavor to honor you always, we don't always, but we will try. We hope after this ends there will be no more tragedy ever. If you need our help as a group, just contact us. Thank you for carrying this message for us.

H: If humanity as a whole only felt what you expressed..... I will convey the message.

If there is nothing else, I bow to each of you and to the spirit of the group which is in the middle of the room. I pull my wings back into my body. I thank the channel. I bow to each of you. Farewell

Animal Spirit Guide Instructions from our member C:

Working with animal energies as totems and guides is a wonderful experience. Knowing and working with your animal totem, or power animal, both have the same meaning; is a valuable gift from the Universe.

In addition to the books listed earlier, you may want to purchase a set of "Medicine Cards" by Jamie Sans & David Carson, which come with a book giving you information on each animal in the deck. While animals and their energy and messages often come and go in our lives as "guides", the following meditation is for meeting your Animal Totem and/or Power Animal. (You can also use this when asking for a totem for guidance and protection for your lightworkers group.) You need only do this simple meditation one time, as your animal totem will not change. Follow the instructions that come with whatever medicine cards you have for cleansing and activating your cards before you use them.

Find a quiet place where you won't be disturbed, and sit comfortably with your medicine cards. If you can be outdoors, all the better. You may want to take a journal to write in, or record your meditation to reference back to for information/messages.

Take a few moments to ground yourself, closing your eyes, take some deep cleansing breaths. Surround yourself with protective energy and love from the Universe. Know that you are safe and protected as you begin your journey to meet your animal totem......

In your mind's eye, begin walking. As you are walking, you will come to a hole in the ground where you are traveling. This hole will be large enough for you to lower yourself into. Reminding yourself that you are totally safe from harm, lower yourself into the hole. See yourself in your mind's eye going down into the earth and traveling, again, completely safe with no issues of breathing or claustrophobia. Notice the walls around you that are the substance of the earth, this is protecting you. Continue walking in this tunnel, until you emerge back out of the earth without any physical or emotional problem.

Take a look at your surroundings, what do you see in your mind's eye? What is the landscape like? Tropical forest? Desert plains? Snow-capped mountains? Rolling hills? Sandy beaches? Is there water around, such as oceans, rivers, streams or lakes? What type, if any, vegetation do you see? Flowers, trees, or grasses? Take note of where you are.

Now, as you look down at your feet, you will see a path. You will begin traveling/walking on that path. Most often, other animals, who could be in the form of insects, reptiles, birds, or fish will make themselves known to you along your journey around this sacred location. If or when you encounter an animal, they are your guide for this journey. Ask them if they have a message for you. If you have your journal, write down the animal and the message(s), or if you are recording repeat the message that you are given. You will most likely be met with more than one guide on this journey, but if not, don't worry. This is a time when you must trust what you are receiving. That is the hardest part of all! Do not allow your logical mind/ego to try to interfere with this part of the meditation. Know that you are on a sacred journey, and the information you are receiving is valid. Don't be surprised if some of the messages are humorous, not everything in the animal spirit world is serious stuff! When you have received the message, offer gratitude to the animal for their message. Continue traveling in your sacred space, making note of any other animals that come across your path and their messages. Do this until you get "that feeling" or "knowing" that your journey has come full circle. You may find yourself back at the place where you emerged from the earth when you arrived in your sacred space.

At this time, offer gratitude for all that has been shown to you. Acknowledge and thank the animal guides that accompanied you on your journey, and the message(s) that you were given. At this time, state that you are ready to meet your animal totem/power animal. If you are back at the place where you emerged from the earth, lower yourself back into the earth, where you are safely led back to your place of meditation, where you started this journey.

As you take a few moments, bring yourself back to this time and place where you are seated comfortably. You feel well rested. Shuffle or spread your medicine cards out. Let your animal totem reveal itself to you in the card that you pull. Again, know that the animal that reveals itself to you IS THE ONE. You may be surprised. You may be confused or disappointed as to what that animal's energy means to you. Look up the information on that animal's energy. Know that this information is meant for you. If things don't "resonate" right away, that's all right. Sit with it for a while, be patient. Messages are revealed when you are meant to receive them. Also, look up the animals that accompanied you on your journey, and see what information they have for you.

You can honor your totem by acquiring an image, be it a picture, statue, etc. and keeping it on your altar, or finding a special place within your home or workplace. You may be surprised when your totem "shows up". Take note of where you are and your surroundings, *what you are doing, and everything going on. Then when you have a quiet moment, connect back with your totem for information, a message or validation.*

On a personal note, trusting the information that I receive from the Universe has always been something I struggle with, although I am getting much better. Shortly after I received my totem "Wolf", I was wondering, "Is this really my totem?" (I mean I was expecting a horse or dog for my totem, as they are physical animals that I have in my life.) Well, that day when I went to get the mail, Wolf made himself/ herself known that YES, I am your totem. A magazine that I get monthly was in the bundle of mail. I opened the first page, and there was a 2-page ad with a wolf in it staring right back at me! AND, also in the bundle was an envelope from Wildlife Federation that was full of address labels with my name and address printed on it with wolf images! Later that evening, watching TV, an ad for a car commercial had a wolf in it. I took a moment later that evening and thanked Wolf for idiot-proofing the validation that I had asked for. That was the last time I questioned if Wolf was my totem. After reading and learning more about Wolf medicine and energy, it has been with me all my life. I wish you the same with your totem.

Your totem can and will let you know it's around or that is has a message for you. While most animals probably won't physically pres- ent themselves to you, it does happen in sacred moments. There are also many other ways that they can make themselves known to you through images in the media like billboards, license plates, music/ sound, etc. Your totem may appear to you in dreams or through just a thought. Trust that they are close at hand and ready to assist you. Just keep your eyes, ears and heart open for them and their message, and don't forget to thank them either!

Janice: We were told in 2012 that a lightworkers handbook needed to be written and suggestions were given by Gaia about what to include. As you can see, this has been a longer time period than we imagined to come to fruition. But, everything in its right time. Shortly after we were given this directive by Gaia, our member C did a channel with the dolphin deva, who had come forward to offer assistance. We had a previous channel from the dolphin deva reminding us to remember 3 things to keep foremost in our lives: 1) Surface and breathe; 2) Stay in your pod (with those that love you); and 3) have fun.

Dolphin Channel

February 24, 2012   Channeled by C

C: Invoking the Dolphin deva. For the purpose of assistance in our lightworkers book, specifically on the animal totem chapter.

Greetings from the sea! I am Miasha. Please relax and enjoy my time with you. It is wonderful that this group is putting this together, for dolphins are most anxious to assist. We are the keepers of the breath, and play. Breath is important to both humans and dolphins, just as is water. Neither species can live without both! Our wish is to see more humans breathe, relax and enjoy the world of all animals, land, sea and air.

We all love humans, and can feel the stresses of your life and what it has become for the human race. Many times we try to offer moments of joy when humans view us in the oceans, showing how playful life should be. We know that when you see us, you are full of wonderment, excitement and joy. There are few of you that can resists us!!

There is much to tell, but I don't want to bog you down with all of it at once, that's not what we are about. We have previously spoken to this group about surfacing to breath as we dolphins do. Many times the human get weighted down by stresses that unknowingly are self-inflicted. By consciously paying attention to the breath, you can alleviate much of this tension. Just think how much the animal kingdom will rejoice when you figure this out and begin to practice it like we do!

C: Miasha what can humans do to gain a connection to a particular totem, to assist them in this?

Miasha: It is as simple as asking for one! Your specific totem or guide can reveal itself to you in your heart, in a quiet moment where of course you are breathing! Many of you will also get other markers of validation through your world via media, tv, books, advertisements, pictures billboards, anywhere around in your day/night. A picture or reminder or the totem itself may show itself to you. But you can't just ask without intention of higher purpose, higher relationship with all living creatures and beings on the planet. We are here to assist, and ready and willing to help our human partners in our universal family, because we are all family, with Gaia/God.

C: Miasha, will humans figure this out?

Miasha: Well, not all will. But you are doing a wonderful things with helping humans to understand how interconnected all life is on this beautiful planet.

Note: C had to take a break and let her dogs out, then came back to this.

C: Stepping aside, opening for the dolphin deva of the seas. Surrounded by white pure energy, stepping away invoking Miasha for assistance, invoking the deva Miasha.

Miasha: Greetings, and yes trust that it is me. So skeptical you are! Thank you for the totem likeness, and no coincidence that it is blue, also part of blue star energy (which we were working with at the time). *Back to animals, yes it is disturbing that you have humans who slaughter. They do not know, you must forgive them.*

C: Why do some humans feel so connected to animals, respect and honor them, when others have none of those feelings?

Miasha: It is part of their humanness so to say. It is the journey of the soul for this time. Many of you are learning, honoring and understanding. From the famous like Caesar Milan (dog whisperer), *yes, the Parelli family* (natural horsemanship), *and Temple Grandin* (animal behaviorist), *who tremendously help with getting humans to learn how animals' psyche work. But even those who have an understanding that are here are helping to teach. This is another reason your lightworkers group is so important. You know when we splash our tails the ripple wave that goes out in the water, it will be a similar effect of your work with in the human family.*

One thing I want to relay; the importance of silence for humans. Communication comes when you are quiet, those are the times when totems can communicate. Too many times humans are so noisy! Make that most of the time! It must be understood that these silent times are so easy, and necessary for this is where the connection is made, the answers are freely given, only to fall on unhearing souls. As we communicate with sound, we do not have all the external disturbances that you have. If the human can just sit quietly for short amounts of time, this is when the light will allow to enter. The light, the universal light. Allowance, forgiveness, silence, trust should be what happens. (Shown light show.) *Enjoy the silence...this is what can happen!* (Then shown a graceful dolphin ballet.)

C: *That was beautiful, thank you.*

Miasha: *You are most welcome. Thank you for the /your silence. As you saw with your third eye, you can also sit quietly with your 2 seeing eyes, and allow them to 'see' the ballet of animals when you sit in silence. It doesn't have to be regimented, it can be as easy as, well, think of it as observing in silence. No need to get hung up on meditation, sometimes that is too heavy for humans. Some are already bogged down, so it can be as light as observing in silence. The animals will show you the beauty and simplicity of their worlds! It will surely be a show for you to remember. Just remember the "dolphins KISS", keep it simply silly. Au revoir!*

C: *Au revoir Miasha. Gratitude and love to you. Closing channel.*

Janice: *As you can see, the messages from animal devas are simple, yet profound. Humans over complicate things, animals show us how to simplify.*

Flower essences

We earlier talked about plants and trees as ancient wisdom guidance, but the use of flower essences has been a constant in human history for eons. Different from herbal remedies, flower essences have been used as medicine on the etheric or energy body more so than the physical body. Humans began being perceived as machines more so than energetic/physical bodies and flower essences began to lose their use with modern day humans. What has been discovered (again) is that our energetic bodies are where healing and balance begin. The Bach Flower Remedies began gaining popular acceptance with the marketing of his 38 essences, but especially of his *Rescue Remedy*, which ended up helping people with anxiety without any side effects.

For group members, doing deep work outside of their comfort zone, flower essences are an excellent way to balance.

Perelandra-Ltd. has flower essences that are especially good for lightworkers. (*I swear they are not paying me to advertise for them!*) Lightworkers often go into altered states for channeling, for journeys, and for grounding energy. Sometimes it can feel like you are trapped in a space between being fully present and out in the ethers someplace. Flower essences are a gentle, natural way to regain that balance. Perelandra has developed rose and other plant essences that are beneficial to this level of lightwork. I am sure there are others that are good as well, but I know that these work.

Janice: I'm not going to spend a lot of time on this, but these essences, in my opinion, are essential for self care after doing intense work, often in unfamiliar realms. I got a couple of sets from Perelandra and after each meeting where we did some deep work, I would muscle test (I use a pendulum) each person for needed flower essences. There are physical changes that take place, in the cranium and spine for instance, when shifting and working with energy. These flower essences help to bring the physical and energetic bodies back into balance. I would suggest you do your own research about what works for you, but I would strongly advocate for using them.

Crystals

We mostly don't think of rocks as having energy. They are rocks. Admittedly, their energy is slower than that of humans or animals or plants, but quite powerful. Each stone or gem or crystal in the mineral kingdom has metaphysical properties. A good resource book to learn about these properties is *Love is in The Earth* by Melody. The down side to this book is that there are no pictures, but you can easily go to the internet to see what they look like. There are a plethora of good books out there, pick one that resonates with you if this one doesn't. Crystals (I'm using this word to represent crystals, stones, rocks, and gemstones) are guides just like animals, trees, and plants. They have their own wisdom and are certainly one of the most ancient forms of life and energy on the Earth. Since everything in existence is simply different patterns of energy, it goes that crystals each possess their own form and vibration.

How are they helpful in lightwork? They can bring energetic assistance when grounding energy for example, or cohesion and intention to a group action. Different crystals resonate with different energy. The best way to begin working with crystals is to just go and buy some and spend some time with them. Every crystal you purchase needs to be cleansed before you begin using it. Some are a high vibration and don't need cleansing, but as a rule, it is a good idea to clean them all.

There are several ways to clean crystals. Keep in mind that some (like selenite and kyanite) are soft and will dissolve in water, so a water bath is not suitable for all crystals. If you don't need them immediately, physically putting them in or on the ground for at least 24 hours, sometimes longer, is a good cleansing and grounding for the stone. Other methods include sea water or salt water immersion (except for the soft stones - always check first); smudging with sage or palo santo; place in a dish of rice and sea salt; rinsing under running water; placing in a potted house plant; sitting them outside for 24 hours in the sun and moon light (full moon is especially good); placing them in or near a singing bowl. Some stones can be cleansed by placing them on another higher vibration crystal. For example, selenite is one of the highest vibration crystals, and you can place other crystals on the selenite and it will clean the lower vibration crystal. It is also important that periodic cleaning be done, especially with those you use the most.

The next step is programming the crystal. If this sound mysterious, it isn't. Programming is merely holding the crystal in your hands and placing your intention into it - tell it what you want it to focus on. The focus can be for healing, for light work, for protection, for guidance and meditation - the important thing is to be clear to the crystal about what you would like it to do. For lightworkers, it is often to act as a guide, or as protection on a journey, or as a conduit for energy you are bringing into the earth.

Pendulums are another good tool for personal use and use in the group. They are usually a crystal of some sort with a chain or cord attached. They are used for simple yes and no answers. When you have found the pendulum that resonates with you, take some time to clean it, program it, and infuse some of your energy into it. This is as simple as just carrying it in your pocket or purse and having contact with it; it makes you into a team. When you are programming the pendulum, ask it to tell you what a "yes" is and what a "no" is. For each of these it will have a different action. The pendulum will either move sideways, up and down, or in a circle to indicate the answer. The "yes" and "no" are different for each person, so there is no wrong or right about how your pendulum will communicate with you. Begin by asking yes and no questions you know the answer to, such as your name, whether you are male/female, children, etc. The action will be clearer the more you use it. It is a good idea to begin your question with "is it in my/the highest good" and that way you can be sure you are getting the answer from your own higher self. Remember that you can't ask questions about anyone but you; if you do ask questions about others, it will only reflect what you think the answer is or should be.

Some crystals are what are called record keepers. These are from ancient civilizations like Lemuria and Atlantis. The wisdom says that as these civilizations were coming to a close, their crystal masters programmed information into certain crystals to be unlocked and used at a future time on Earth. When used in meditation, they can open to vast stores of information that will be helpful to a lightworker group. Atlantean generally have arrow shapes either embedded into the crystal or raised on it; Lemurian have striations along the side of the crystal. Let yourself be guided intuitively to the one or ones that are needed for your journey or the journey of your group.

Crystal grids are another tool that can be made for specific purposes. These can be useful to enhance the power of crystals - more are naturally more powerful than one or two. For personal use, they can be for empowerment, healing, attracting love or abundance, etc. For use in a lightworker group, they take on a larger role. If your group knows it is going to be doing some deeper energy work, it may be helpful for each person to pick a crystal and make it part of a grid with the intention that the grid bring the group energy together for this higher purpose. This way, energetically the group is already cohesive before the work ever begins. Often they are laid out in geometric patterns (patterns can be found on the internet), for a more intentional effect. A bigger stone like a quartz point or sphere is often used in the center as a starting point and it serves to activate the grid. There are instructions below on how to set up a grid.

This is just a short overview of crystals, much more information can be found on the internet or in books. They are essential for doing light work.

Janice: My knowledge and use of crystals was very limited when I first came into my lightworkers group. I always liked rocks and had a rock tumbler as a kid. I just didn't know why I liked them. The longer I was in the group, the more attracted I became to crystals. I was so fortunate to have training from an Indian crystal master when I first began doing hypnotherapy. He introduced me to crystals and how they could assist my clients in their healing process. I keep a basket of crystals in my office and let my clients select a stone to hold during their session. Of course, these are selected by me to be the best ones for healing and programmed to assist people in their healing journey.

Our group was fortunate to have a woman who is the most knowledge-able person I've seen in knowing about and using crystals. Two other members were also very well versed and it was a wonderful learning experience for the rest of us, plus a powerful tool in our toolbox to have all this knowledge and skill at our fingertips. Even if your group doesn't start out with this good fortune, members will learn and grow together. This group member didn't join until our fourth or fifth year in existence and we all learned together as we went along before that.

As I've said before, trust yourself. This applies to crystals as well as everything else. My best way to pick a stone is to hold them in my hand and notice how it feels. If there are several of the same kind, I will pick each one up and hold it and compare them until I find the one that feels best to me. If I am still unsure, I will use my pendulum for confirmation.

From our member L, these are instructions on how to set up a crystal grid.

Crystal Grids are intentional arrangements of crystals, minerals, stones and other organic materials that direct energies toward a specific purpose.

Anyone can make one. Here are the step-by-step instructions:

1. *Start with a purpose. Your purpose can be as simple as global awareness or as specific as sending healing energy to a sick friend. Any pure intention will do.*

2. *Gather your materials. Select an assortment of crystals, minerals or organic materials while keeping your intention in mind. You can begin with a main crystal and surrounding stones. I have been known to use crystals, flower heads, tamarind seeds, sea shells, and feathers all in the same grid.*

3. *Find a location for your grid. I like to use a flat square plate, round plant base, piece of glass or stone slab. I use it strictly for grid work. I call it the Plate of Intention.*

4. *Clean, cleanse and clear your space. Make sure your area / Plate of Intention is clean, dust free. Cleanse your area with incense, smoke, or salt water. Clear your space by smudging with sage or saying a prayer. You can also burn candles, play music, or tone to add to your grid experience.*

5. *Set your intention. Breathe. Think about your intention. Visualize the situation. Complete the intention by visualizing the desired outcome. Be clear. Be true. Be pure with your intention.*

6. *Lay out your grid. You can begin with a geometric structure or symbol. Start with something that resonates with you or your purpose. This may change as you create your grid. Lay out the stones. I like to go clockwise as if building, spiraling, spinning like a helix. Let it flow. It's a symbiotic relationship.*

It is an energy exchange - there are no limitations. Your particular creativity is most important. Let your intuition guide you. Once your stones, minerals etc. are in place set your main crystal in the middle.

7. *Connect to your grid. Visualize the outcome of your intention. Touch your third eye, heart, or throat and touch the center stone. Feel the energy resonate between you and the grid. This completes the circle manifesting your intention. Breathe.*

8. *Say a prayer of Gratitude. You may even meditate or tone, whatever feels right. Enjoy the feeling!*

Notes: Get caught up in the details. These grids can be simple or elaborate depending on your vision. Enjoy the process. These methods help to open your energy centers to life force energies and open the mind to new levels of consciousness.

Energy

Working with energy is the crux of what lightwork is about. If you are looking for measurable and tangible results, this may not be the work for you. One must have a great deal of trust in the process and the group to be successful.

It would stand to reason that many of the group members will the empaths - ones that can feel the energy of a person or place. Using this intuitive ability helps the group to navigate what "feels" right to work on and to feel the difference when the work is complete. This is also where trust comes in; you have to trust your own energy to discern if the time is right to work on something, or if it is time to back off.

This is where the discussion comes in about light (high vibration) energy and dark (lower vibration) energy. They are both very real energies and, with practice, it will become fairly easy to know which is which. For instance, one would expect the energies to be very different between a high vibration/holy place (church, shrine, etc.) and a lower vibration place (prison, bar, etc.). For practice, let yourself go to places you would expect high or low vibrations and just sit with it for a while to notice how the energy feels and how it is different. Also remember that not all dark is low vibration – we can't see the stars without the darkness. It is more about vibration than about light/dark.

There are many high vibrational energies that are interesting in working with lightworker groups and it will depend on your group who you turn to. These can be ascended masters like Jesus, Buddha, Krishna, Kwan Yin, and others; they can be from the angelic realm like any of the Archangels, Cherubim or Seraphim; they can be other civilizations like the Pleadians, Sirians, or Council of Elohim; they can be crystals like selenite, elestial quartz, danburite, indigo gabbro, and others; trees and plants such as giant redwoods, sequoias, roses; animals/animal devas such as white lions, eagles/hawks, whales/dolphins, elephants. Try them all out to see which ones resonate with you and/or your group.

In contrast, there are low vibrational energies that are also attracted to light emanating from a lightworker group. (We will discuss protection in the next section.) Please be assured this is not a judgement, these energies have chosen to stay at this level and that may be appropriate for their karmic path at this time. That being said, these are not the energies a lightwork group needs or wants to have inserting itself. Especially at first, when energy is called in, let the group sit with it for a few minutes to assure that everyone feels it is appropriate.

Janice: When our group began, we were about half and half with who was familiar with energy work and who wasn't. We had several reiki practitioners in the group who were accustomed to energy work, so they were quite comfortable. As I said earlier in the book, one of the first things we did as a group was to have one person sit in the center while everyone else sent them energy. This accomplished two things - first for the group to practice sending energy, and second for them to feel what positive incoming energy felt like.

Practice is the real key to working with energy. Some good group exercises:

~Have each member individually sit with something in nature - a tree, a bird, a body of water, etc. and allow a message to come;

~In group meeting or individually, have several different crystals available of differing vibrations (ex: selenite, granite, amethyst, etc.) and have each person hold each stone and see if they can determine the different vibrations as they are held;

~During a meditative time, call in Archangel Michael, then Kwan Yin, then the whale deva, etc. to feel the difference in the energies.

~I do not suggest calling in lower vibrational energies. After you have been exposed to the higher vibrations, the lower ones will be readily apparent.

Protection

Okay, no need to freak out. The bogey man is not out to get you. For the most part, whenever you are doing lightwork, you are protected by your own guides and those of your group. When you have your opening circle, the energy formed around the group is high vibration and protective. As I mentioned previously, the light will attract some lower vibrational energies and this is about keeping those apart from your own energy and that of the group.

There are a number of ways to protect yourself and your group. One way is to simply ask for protection from whomever your source energy is - God, angels, Mohammed, Gaia, et. al. Another is to program crystals for that purpose. Some good protection crystals are black tourmaline, smokey quartz, amethyst, peridot, black obsidian; or a crystal grid can be made for protection. Smudging with sage or palo santo - the room and even each person - can remove any negative energy.

Janice: This is one of those things that we don't always consciously do as a group at this point in time, but one that is important especially early on before you know the personalities of the group and their history. The example I want to give you from our group is of a younger woman who was working through some childhood abuse issues with a therapist. At one of our meetings, she had an outburst where she was angry and yelling because of the direction of the group. This was not her normal demeanor, so it was quite upsetting. Because she was in such a negative space in her therapy, we talked privately after the meeting and it was agreed that the group was not the right place for her at that time. In hindsight, it was clear to me that for a couple of months leading up to this that she was bringing in negativity and energetically disrupting the group and our work.

We have recently started sometimes doing crystal grids for protection, mostly because we are working on an energetic and vibrational plane we have not delved into before. We have been asked to do some work that is unfamiliar and it feels pertinent to institute protection before we go into the unknown. In truth, we probably don't need it, but it makes us feel better and safer. And it really is about how comfortable you feel doing the work.

Chapter 10:

THE IMPORTANCE OF CEREMONY

Ritual and ceremony have been part of the human experience since the dawn of time. It is ingrained in our DNA. Whether it is saying a prayer at bed or meal times, wearing your lucky shirt for the big game, making coffee as soon as you get out of bed, or saying marriage vows publicly, so many things in our lives follow guidelines established by us or by a person or institution important to us. It gives us comfort with the sometimes uncomfortable, and certainty when other things in our lives may be uncertain.

Earlier in this book I outlined some things to do as a group when you are starting out - the opening and closing circles, the check-ins, and pot-luck food after the meeting. Each group will find its own rituals that become important. Solstices, equinoxes, eclipses, full and new moons, or any natural phenomenon offer opportunities to build ceremony around. For instance, there are groups that capture the energy of the solstice or equinox with ribbons or other objects to use with the group work; there are groups who meet at specific power locations at certain times that are important to the group; there may be times of the year set up for retreats or other bonding experiences. If there is a labyrinth nearby, the group may sometimes want to walk that together for cohesion and clarity.

Anything that your group decides is important to build ceremony around is what you should do. Maybe celebrating birthdays is important, or marking the anniversary of the group start as a celebration day - whatever you decide, is entirely appropriate to your group. This may seem like a little or inconsequential thing, but it is one of those things that enforces group cohesion.

Janice: This is a hard one to explain, but one I think is important enough to include. We know that when our group meets, we will have an opening circle and then we will check in, and the meeting will have a closing circle. It may seem silly, but it is continuity no matter how the group evolves. For many, this is familiar and comfortable, especially when you and your group are doing unfamiliar and uncomfortable work.

Early on, I read in one of Machelle Small Wright's books (really, I swear she is not paying me!) about how she uses ribbon to collect energy from the solstice, so our group tried it. We then cut it up and each person got a piece, and we used it personally and in the group for supportive energy. I still carry several of my ribbon pieces in my purse and it feels reassuring to have that piece of group energy always with me.

One of our first ceremonies was at the labyrinth at R's house when we were asked to download some blue-star energy. We had no idea what we were doing, but making the task into a ceremony seemed to help us be more comfortable with it. One by one we filed into the labyrinth and stopped at the point that felt right for us to stand - we were each at a different place in the labyrinth, and as the facilitator I was in the middle. I called the energy to come in through each of us, activated by our hearts, and then each person sent the energy into the ground. Each of us felt supported by the others, with no position being any more important than another. When it was complete, we filed out in the order which we entered. Because we felt that this ceremony went well, it translated into a level of comfort with the work we were doing, and with each other. .

Chapter 11:

HOW TO GROUND ENERGY

What does it even mean to ground energy? When the group is made aware, through a channel or some other means, that new or different energy needs to be added to the earth energy, then it is appropriate to receive and ground it.

In the previous chapter I spoke about gathering energy in objects or in places like a labyrinth. It usually becomes apparent through a message of some sort to a group member that there is energy waiting to be received. As planets and galaxies spin, new doorways are opened and new energy is available to help the planet and her inhabitants. Most often it needs to come through a human body and, more specifically, through a human heart. The human heart imbibes the energy with a connection, much like a plug going into an electrical socket. The energy exists in the wall socket, and is needed in the electronic device, but it needs to be plugged in for it to work. It is the same principle with grounding energy. There are many websites that talk about these special times of energy influx, many happen during eclipses, solstices, equinoxes and other natural phenomena - examples of these websites are those of Elizabeth Peru and Lee Harris, but you may find your own. Group discussion is encouraged to evaluate if a particular energy is right for your group to work with.

As with everything else, your intention to do good work means everything. If you don't get the technique just right, it still counts.

The most common way to ground energy is to receive it into your left (receiving) hand and discharge it out through your right (sending) hand. This can be done with just your hands, or with the aid of crystals, which amplify the energy. For example, you may want to choose a stone such as selenite, kyanite, or elestial quartz for receiving the energy, and a stone such as garnet, petrified wood, or shungite for sending or grounding the energy. There are many other stones available and suitable, these are just suggestions. Simply point the left hand upward and ask that the energy be downloaded, then allow it to pass through your heart. Next point the right hand toward the ground and ask that the energy be sent into the earth.

If your guidance says that the energy needs to be grounded in a specific place for a longer period of time, it may be appropriate to "plant" a stone there. I have heard of several shaman who go around the world leaving stones in specific places to connect the energy and keep it grounded. In areas where there has been conflict, sorrow, or other deep negative emotion, a planted crystal may help with long-term clearing. Planting a crystal is exactly what it says, physically digging a hole in a place that feels right or has been agreed upon by the group, and placing the crystal in the hole and covering it. Intention should be placed or programmed with the stone to act as an energy center for the earth and all inhabitants.

Sometimes an energy vortex needs to be created in a certain space. These tend to bring up the vibration of the space where they are located. There are many naturally-occurring vortexes in existence, most notably at sacred sites around the world - Machu Picchu, Mount Shasta, Stonehenge, and The Great Pyramid to name just a few. These energy vortexes are connected by what are called energy ley lines. It is where these ley lines meet that vortexes naturally occur. The more vortexes and ley lines, the more the earth, humans, and all earth inhabitants will benefit from this higher vibration.

On a side note, raising the energy of water can also be a powerful tool. Water can be collected from any natural place - the ocean, a pond, or river - and the higher vibration energy can be funneled into the collected water. My friend, who literally is a rocket scientist, tells me that this is called population inversion. The lower vibrational atoms will raise themselves to match higher vibrational atoms in the same area. When the collected water is energized, it can be released back into the place it came from, or a similar salinity of water (don't put ocean water into a fresh water source), and it will gradually affect the entire body of water. Potentially this higher vibrational water can be spread into even drinking water supplies, giving humans yet another way to raise vibration.

Janice: Our first energy grounding was in the labyrinth that I previously described. We had no idea what we were doing; our member R did a channel from Gaia saying that Blue Star energy was beaming toward the earth and we needed to receive and ground it. We talked about it and agreed that we would use the technique I've described to you, but using our hands and not crystals (we weren't quite there yet with the crystals). The Gaia channel was how we learned the energy needed to be activated by a human heart. That same channel told us there was a ley line just about 20' off the beach in our North Carolina coastal location that ran directly into Washington, DC. Good energy going into Washington? Yes please!

We did some research about Blue Star energy and found information about it in old Hopi prophecies. This was the energy to usher in the new age and it was important that groups work to bring it in. Now that we have passed the 2012 shift, that energy no longer (at least for us) needs to be introduced.

We found that with the series of eclipses in 2016, things shifted in the universe to allow a new source of energy to appear. This is when we have started using crystals to assist us. The crystals we used were blue kyanite to receive, and garnet to ground. I nearly always experience a sensation like a very mild electric current moving through my body. It doesn't hurt at all, but feels like when you are tingly and twitchy with excitement. I'm including this so you don't freak out if this happens to you. I wondered at first if I was having a mild seizure, but my friend the rocket scientist explained that it is the body's reaction to an electric current moving through it. Any time you touch even a mild electric current; the body twitches naturally. As you adjust to receiving energy, this will become less. I barely notice it these days when I am grounding energy. I thought at first the new energy was more subtle, but I realized I am just more experienced and have raised my own vibration enough so that it doesn't affect me that way any more. This seems to be true for our entire group.

Chapter 12:

PHYSICAL CHANGES

I include this because as you go more deeply into lightwork, the body has to shift and change to accommodate different energy. If our bodies did not change, the incoming energy would likely cause us to explode! A container can only hold so much energy before it bursts, so as new energy comes in and is grounded, old energy has to leave. This is what causes physical symptoms to appear, just the body's way of cleaning house. A little disclaimer first, if you feel like you need medical attention, please get it. This is meant only as a guide to changes that may be experienced. Western medicine is a good thing when you need it.

There are a lot of manifestations of these physical changes. Some sources talk about the "ascension flu", which are flu-like symptoms when energy gets ramped up or big energetic changes are happening. As the body is infused with more and more light energy, the older and lower vibrational energy has to be eliminated. That can be experienced as a sore and achy body, fever and hot/cold chills, respiratory issues, headaches, dizziness, nausea, tiredness and lethargy, just like when you have a bad case of the flu. Other symptoms that may not be flu-like include heart palpitations, especially in the area just above the heart (thymus), ringing in the ears, hot flashes and excessive sweating (especially at certain times of the day), excessive energy or overwhelming fatigue, gas or bloating, and scalp tingling.

To put this in terms that might be better understood, it's as if you're trying to run a Windows Vista program on a Windows 11 computer. You have to upgrade or it won't work any more. It will still run the old programs, but nothing new can be added because it is incompatible. The software upgrade does not change the physical properties of the computer, but only the internal processes. In order to upgrade the computer, as the new software is introduced, it takes a little time for the computer to be offline while the processor is being upgraded. We are electrical beings, so the process is essentially the same.

If you start experiencing any of these symptoms, there are a couple of things I would suggest. First is to check online and see what is happening energetically - there will always be buzz in the online spiritual community about celestial events such as eclipses, moon phases, solstices, eclipses, etc. as well as information about new sources of energy influx. Check with other members of your group to see if they are having similar symptoms, usually others are experiencing the same or similar types of things. Rest, rest, rest. Listen to your body, if it tells you to slow down and rest, do it. You're trying to rev the engine of a vehicle low on gas. It will work for a little while, but if you don't stop, it will cease operation. It won't kill you, but most likely you will get sick or sustain some sort of injury that makes you be still.

Other good ways to help with this are using flower essences, drinking lots of water, meditation, and grounding in nature (bare feet on the ground or hugging a tree), And rest!

The chakra system in the body is what moves the energy, so it is important to keep your chakras aligned and clear. If you don't know what chakras are or how they work, there is a lot of information out there to read, so I won't go into that here. Suffice to say that it is important to regularly clear them.

A couple of ways will work. A meditation, guided or silent, Chakras are like little fans aligned inside the body. Familiarize yourself with the colors and during your meditation focus on each color from the base chakra to the crown. As you focus on each area and color, you can see, feel, or imagine that vibrant color and any discolorations being swept away by the fan until it is clear. The energy of white light running through them all and connecting them at the end will seal and protect them. Another way is to get a crystal or stone for each chakra (often you can find them in sets) and lie down and place them on each chakra center. Let these stay in place for 15-30 minutes and they will naturally clear your chakras. There are also practitioners you can pay to do this for you.

The high heart or thymus, and the high crown chakras are being activated over the past several years and most informational sites don't include them because they are not the traditional seven that most know about. The color for the high heart is turquoise, and the high crown is iridescent white or clear (like a clear quartz). Add these into your chakra clearing routine. The high heart is activating intuition and compassion, and the high crown is activating connection to the higher self and the larger universe.

The last thing I want to mention is ringing in the ears. This is different from tinnitus because it is not constant, but rather short bursts of sounds, usually high pitched, but not always. These usually last 15-50 seconds but have been known to last longer. Sometimes they are infrequent and random, and sometimes they are in rapid succession over a shorter time period. These are messages received directly by your brain or pineal gland and decoded there. Pay attention to what you are doing or what you were thinking before it happened as a clue to what it may be about. Differing sources have different theories and you need to use your own guidance about which of these theories resonates with you.

Janice: This is one of those things that we were all surprised about. When we started our group, no one had heard of ascension flu or any of these other symptoms. The first time I had heart palpitations I was very concerned and in talking with one of the other group members I mentioned it. She immediately said "ME TOO" and we both expressed relief as we compared symptoms. It happened to be during a solstice time as I recall, and we put it together and went searching and found that this was a common symptom. Our group has a secret Facebook page and we now know if one of us is having symptoms, we post it on that page so others will know they are not imagining their own symptoms.

I know I said several times to rest, but I mean it - experience speaking here! I have learned over time that when I start experiencing these things, it is time to slow it down and rest as much as possible. I know we all have lives to lead, but build in as much down time as possible when your body tells you to. Being the hard-headed individual I can sometimes be, I told myself to just push through a little harder and not be such a whiny baby. It doesn't work. When I have ignored the messages from my body and usually a little nudge from my guides, I end up getting sick for real or throwing out my back or twisting my ankle, etc., etc. "OK" the universe says to me, "if you won't do what we ask, we will make you do it anyhow." Believe me, it is far easier and less painful to willingly participate.

When I moved to Santa Fe, NM from Kitty Hawk, NC, my body had a lot of adjustments to make. I went from a 4' elevation to a 7000' elevation and from high to low humidity. I knew I was in the right place because spirit had guided me there. What came next was an influx of new energy and new directives about jobs for our group. I had all things respiratory for a couple of years, and every time I decided it was time to move forward because I was tired of waiting, the universe would virtually hit me in the head with a 2x4 again to tell me "not yet". The point of this is that our bodies have to have time to process, and each body is different. What is two years for me may be two months for you. Just listen to your body. This is the instrument you will use for years to come in your lightwork, so you must take care of it. I won't be telling you how to eat or drink or exercise or what body type you should have. You know what is right for you.

Part Three:

THE ONGOING GROUP

Chapter 13:

CONFLICT RESOLUTION

It is inevitable that there will be times when members disagree, it is human nature. As my mama used to say, "you can disagree without being disagreeable". This is another reason it is important early on to establish good communication and cohesion within the group. This is also why it is good to have retreat times and meetings without a work agenda, so that matters can be brought up and resolved before they blow up.

At meetings where there is no agenda or work to be done, ask for members to share where they see the group heading and ask if they are satisfied with their role and level of participation. A note can be sent out in advance if desired to allow folks to think about the questions and be prepared to discuss their thoughts and feelings at the meeting or retreat. If there are any problems or concerns, that is the time to address them.

As I have suggested before, it is, I believe, necessary for the facilitator to maintain contact with each person individually. As part of that, allow them a safe space to bring up concerns or disagreements that are bothering them without making it into a gossip session. If you know all the sides to a story, you are more likely to be able to suggest a talk between the ones have a disagreement with common ground they can consider. If the parties are unwilling to communicate, there is nothing you can do about that. In my experience, if it comes down to one person being unwilling to communicate, they will likely be leaving the group of their own accord.

There are also tools that can be used to encourage communication. Having each person draw a tarot or other kind of deck card can open dialogue just by having that person explain why they think they drew that card and how it relates to them personally and with the group. A traditional Native American talking stick can be used. Whomever is holding the stick is the only one who can talk without being interrupted. When they are finished, they hand the stick (or any object) to the next person.

I don't encourage third person participation unless it is a professional. Sometimes a well-meaning person can appear to be more on one side or another and make the conflict even worse. They are grown-ups and need to sort things out themselves, and it is OK to tell them that.

Sometimes, as the facilitator, all a group member needs to do is be heard, and you can be that person. Often just listening and perhaps pointing out a different perspective can be all the resolution that is needed. Frequently a solution will appear as the situation is talked out calmly.

If there is an outburst or open conflict in the setting of a meeting, it is up to the facilitator to stop it in whatever way possible. Ask the parties if they want to discuss it calmly then, and if they don't, close the meeting as soon as possible and allow everyone time to cool off and think more clearly. If the meeting moves forward with the parties willing to calmly discuss things, be aware of the participation of other members. They can made wonderful suggestions and act as liaisons in conflict resolution, or they can make a bad situation even worse. It is up to the facilitator to make the call.

All this being said, conflicts rarely happen because of the nature of the group. People are there to do work on a higher plane and are usually willing and able to resolve issues quickly and peacefully.

Janice: In the history of our group, I can only think of a couple of times this has happened. At the time I'm writing this, it has been over 15 years, so not a bad record.

The main concerns have been about meeting attendance (too many meetings missed/not making the meetings a priority), meeting content (too overwhelming/not doing enough), and personality issues (talking over top of each other/not being respectful of other opinions or offering unsolicited opinions).

We did have a member who had an outburst at one of the meetings about meeting content and how she wasn't happy with the direction. We were all surprised about it because she had talked to no one about her concerns. As the facilitator, I talked to her the next day and asked about what had spurred this outburst. She was one of our younger members and ultimately I think she felt very constrained by the group and ready to resign, but due to her inexperience didn't know how to leave without creating a reason. She later wrote an apology to the group and all parted on good terms.

On another occasion, two members had a conflict outside of the group and consequently were not speaking to each other. One member elected to take a sabbatical for a couple of months to see if they could resolve the issue without bringing it into the group dynamics. They were unable to resolve the issue and the member who went on sabbatical ended up leaving the group. I talked to both parties and heard both sides. One was willing to talk it out, one was not. In a case like this, there is nothing that can be done by the facilitator or the group.

One member had an issue going to another member's house for the meetings. There was a situation she didn't like to see, which the other member whose house it was didn't see an issue with. The solution was that the member with the issue used Skype to come to the meetings. There were no hard feelings on either side, but an acknowledgment that they had different thoughts about the situation, and agreed to disagree - without being disagreeable.

We have had few conflicts in the group an I suspect the same will be true for most groups given the nature of why the group is in existence. Some problems will find a solution, some with not. All you can do is your best as a facilitator or a group member to help resolve it, and if it cannot be resolved, to accept the outcome.

Chapter 14:

INVOLVING EACH MEMBER OF THE GROUP

Each group member needs to feel as if they are an integral part of contribution to the mission. Some will take a more active role than others based on their skill set and level of comfort and experience. As we discussed previously, some members will come with a lot of experience and some will come with none. Members should be encouraged to participate, whatever their level of skill. If they seem hesitant, the facilitator can contact them outside of the meeting time to figure out why. Some folks will be intimidated by those who have a larger skill set (through no fault of other group members) and afraid of appearing foolish. A good facilitator can help the person feel more at ease about their place. This is, in part, why the group needs to take time to let new members integrate.

A good way to help members involve is to carefully make sure each person has a turn in closing the meeting, and not choosing the same people every time. You could even ask that each person be prepared to do a closing should they be invited to do so.

This was mentioned before, but it bears repeating. Everyone is good at something and asking them to step up for a meeting and do a presentation to the group will help them feel more involved and more connected. It is easy to get complacent about this, especially if the group has been together for a while. Even if a person is not well versed in a particular subject, it will help them, and the group, for them to do some research and present their findings. This is a good way to explore things that the group may be interested in but not knowledgeable about. There is no limit to subject matter available for group learning and exploration.

Janice: I will admit this is something we have not been good about over the years and I suspect some members of the group have drifted away because they felt like they were not contributing. This is one of the reasons for writing this book, so that your group has a little heads-up about things that could have been done differently if we had any idea what we were doing.

Over the past year or two, we have been much better about this. We have had presentations about toning and chanting, creating boxes to collect found items that are sacred, meanings about shapes of crystals and how it affects their use, reviews of spiritual conferences and retreats that were attended, journaling about special contacts with the natural world, and even about aliens. I learn something every single time.

I do want to stress that although these learning opportunities are a great way to increase knowledge and develop group cohesion, the main purpose is of service and lightwork. But, for times when work needs to slow down or stop for any number of reasons, these are a good way to promote continuity.

An additional thing we do each year is to have each member of the group reaffirm themselves to the group mission and to making the group a priority. I feel that saying out loud that you are committing yourself to this work makes a difference in your level of interest and of feeling like you are part of the group.

Chapter 15:

MOVING FORWARD OR TIME TO DISBAND THE GROUP

There may be times in the life of the group when it feels stale or stagnant, or that you are doing the same thing over and over. When the group hits those snags, it is time to sit down and talk about why this is happening and what to do about it. It could be that some members are more active than others and feel they are carrying the group. It could be that some may feel that they have nothing more to learn or to offer and the meetings are a waste of time. Perhaps the number of participants is so small that you feel ineffective in your tasks. There are any number of reasons for a group to hit the wall.

When these times occur, your group is at a crossroads. There are new directions that can be taken, although not everyone may feel comfortable with some of these new directions. Care should be taken to include the thoughts and feelings of all members and to back away from things that are out of anyone's comfort zone. Or, it may just be time to end if you feel like the group has done all it was supposed to, or if there is no energy or interest in moving in new directions.

Just like in any relationship, it takes work and planning to keep things fresh and to choose over and over again to remain in the relationship and nourish it to the best of your ability. And just like in any relationship, it is sometimes in the highest good to end it.

Ending the group is just like any individual member leaving - there should be no blame or hard feelings, just a loving release of something once held dear. A ceremony can be planned to energetically and physically separate. Especially if a group has been together for any length of time, there is an energetic signature that identifies the group and you as a member of that group. By consciously separating each person from that energy, it will cease to exist and group members will be released from it.

This doesn't mean that you can't remain friends, or even occasionally work together on a specific project, but the dynamic of the group is dissolved and participants are released.

Janice: Since our group formed, we have been through several of these, what I like to call, reorganizations. It usually occurs for us when we have completed a task or project we have been working on for a while. It is at these endings that some people chose to leave the group, and some people rededicated to finding the next project we were to be tasked with.

The best example I can think of is when we were working with Blue Star energy frequently before the 2012 shift. We loved ourselves some Blue Star energy and got very familiar with how to use and direct it. When the shift occurred, it was no longer needed, it had done its job. We were a little at a loss of what to do next. For a couple of months as I recall, we felt like we were adrift and without purpose. When we finally made a point to talk about it, we went to our sources of guidance to find what was next. A couple of people did elect to end their participation then, and we lovingly released them. For nearly two years, there were only four of us in the group and we moved forward in different directions we were all comfortable with.

As much as I loved that time with the intimacy of the small group, it became time to add new members more aligned with our new direction. Some were content with the changes, and some eventually left as other new members arrived.

It is my belief that the group always has the members that are there to do the specific work we are tasked with. There have been several folks I have been heartsick to see leave, but for whatever reasons, it was their time to go. And I had to let them go.

For me, this group is like the air I breathe, I cannot imagine my life without it. I feel nourished and understood and accepted by the other members, and it is one of the very few places I feel safe to express exactly who I am and whatever I am experiencing. There are other members that feel the same way. Because of this, there has never been a time when we have talked about disbanding the group. I can't say it will never happen, there may be a time that our work is no longer needed. I don't see that in the foreseeable future, but it could happen. It is the way I feel I am making a difference in the world, even if no one sees it.

Chapter 16:

IT'S NOT FOR EVERYONE

There will be some that read this that say to themselves, "has this woman lost her ever-loving mind?" These thoughts and concepts will be so totally foreign that it will be lumped in with sci-fi fantasy or a mental disorder. If you have read this far, you are probably not that person.

There will be those who read this and say to themselves, "hallelujah I'm not the only one!" Those people will find relief that there are others out there like them and they can know they are not alone. When you are in a location or situation where you think and believe differently than the people around you, it can be very isolating. You may even wonder if there is something wrong with you. Believe me, most of us have been there if we are on a lightworker path.

There may be long time friends or family members that turn away from you or put distance in your relationship. Some will walk away from your life completely and you will have to let them go. Some will not know why, but they will know that you have changed and the relationship doesn't feel right any more. There will be those that accuse you of thinking you are better than everyone else, or that you are on a dangerous and cult-like path. There is nothing you can do or say that will satisfy these people and it is best to not waste time and energy trying to convince them otherwise. My advice is to listen and thank them for their concern and then zip your lips.

This path takes courage and a willingness to go beyond your comfort zone. It will take you to places you never dreamed of going and will push you to find places within yourself that you didn't know existed. You will discover gifts that have been hiding deep inside that have just been waiting for the right time and the right group of people to be revealed. There will be times of doubt and times of exhilaration, but it will never be boring.

If this resonates with you, perhaps it is time for you to start looking for your people. Even if it resonates with you and you do not find a group, you can still do lightwork. As I have read time and again, and have been told by my guides and through channels, if you don't do anything but stand still and shine your light, it is enough.

Janice: I remember the exact time I knew I was a lightworker. I was in the mountains of Virginia taking hypnotherapy master's training. One segment involved using the hypnotic state to help remove attached spirits from a person's energy field. Prior to the training I had read a book about it and frankly, it scared the living daylights out of me. We spent an entire day learning and training to do this work. As most everyone in the class was giving it a "no thank you", I began to know with certainty that I was meant to do this work. I knew I would have to go out of my comfort zone, and trust that guidance and skills would come. The instructor indicated that this work was done by lightworkers. I hadn't heard the term before and decided if that is what a lightworker was, then I guess I was one.

During the course of this awakening and claiming who I really was, I lost friends along the way, including friends that had been there all of my life. They didn't understand the change and thought I had gone off the deep end. My attempts at trying to explain myself resulted in being laughed at sometimes, being told I was not living the kind of life I was supposed to be, or that I needed to "see someone" about what was going on. Sometimes it was hurtful, sometimes it felt good to drop the drama and the baggage. It gets easier with time. Don't doubt yourself if you have chosen this path.

Somewhere in the back of my mind, there is a little fear that when people I know read this book, I will be totally and completely exposed. I suspect some past life experiences of being killed for doing this kind of work are in there somewhere. But part of me is happy that I won't have to hide who I really am any more. It will be out there for everyone to see. I hope people will be kind, but even if they aren't, I am who I am – and you are who you are. Own it.

Part Four:

CONCLUSION

BRINGING IN THE LIGHT

Chapter 17:

CONCLUSION

Congratulations! You made it all the way through and didn't run away screaming.

This subject is so dear to my heart and I wish I had been able to read something like this when we were starting out with our group. This originally came up years ago as "circles of seven" from a regression one of my clients did. I looked everywhere for information about these circles and what they were and how to form them. There was nothing. I had been to Mt. Shasta at a Kryon conference, and got an opportunity to talk to Lee Carroll, the original Kryon channel. I asked him about these circles and he said he had heard of something like it, but nothing specifically. Then he suggested that perhaps I was the one that should write the book. I was not doing any writing at that time and scoffed at the idea that I would be able to do that. But I never forgot those words.

There are always defining moments in our lives that show or tell us exactly who we are; they can be embraced or declined. My experience is that if you are truly meant to do something, it will keep coming up over and over until you give up and embrace it. Sometimes you will get glimpses of it before it is time to be embraced just to start preparing you for what is to come. You don't have to jump into it all at once, you can start reading and learning and just finding out what resonates with you and what doesn't. I would encourage you to read books, listen to podcasts, watch videos, and talk to people. Gather a range of information and sources and trust yourself to know what feels right, what resonates, and what doesn't. This is a good way to start defining to yourself, who you are.

Take classes if you can. I was fortunate enough to live close to the Association for Research and Enlightenment (ARE) in Virginia Beach, home of Edgar Cayce and his work. They have week- long classes and weekend classes to help hone your skills, and to figure out what those skills are. I know there are many wonderful places like this around the country, and world, but ARE was what resonated with me. There are like-minded people in these places where you can discuss what you are doing and get feedback and information. You may even find some of your group members there.

When you decide to start your group, be confident and courageous. Sometimes seeing someone like that will empower others to come out of their shells and join you. As long as your intention is for your highest good and the highest good of those around you, there is no fail, there is no wrong way to do this.

Even if you are just standing still, your shining light will change the world.

Remember to keep an open mind,
Remember to keep an open heart,
Remember to stay open to all possibilities.

Part Five:

CHECKLIST FOR GETTING STARTED

- Think about who would be a good fit for this group
- Brainstorm with a few people to determine who to invite
- Set up one person as the group facilitator
- Issue invitations to those who have made the list
- Set the time, place, and date for the first meeting
- At the first meeting, ask for a commitment or decline before the next meeting date
- Follow up with interested participants before the next meeting
- Establish an opening ritual
- Start and end meetings on time
- Create group energy and cohesiveness through sharing personal journeys
- Develop a group mission statement
- Encourage people to define their roles and contributions
- Get input from the group about what kind of social interaction is preferred
- Make an effort to get to know each member of the group individually
- Make a plan for how often you will have retreats and set a date
- How would you like to formally end the meetings
- With input from everyone, decide what you would like to start working on
- Create a list of "projects" and ideas
- Decide what you will focus on for the next meeting
- Have fun

Welcome lightworker! You have read the book and now you are ready to begin your journey. Congratulations on your decision to bring more light into our world.

This segment is meant to help you stay organized and focused on the tasks at hand. Rather than having to keep referencing the book, this is laid out so that you can make notes and have them all in one place. Remember, these are only suggestions and if you have a different or better way of doing things, by all means use your own intuition and guidance.

Part One: Getting Started

Begin by getting together with a small group to get a list together of who to invite.

Who are these folks?

Name	Phone	Email Address

Initial meeting information:

Where?

When (Date and Time)?

Great! You have set up your initial meeting and it is now time to discuss who to invite to the first meeting of the full group. Take some time to brainstorm and talk about who you each may know that has an interest in this sort of gathering or has talent that you think may be a good fit for the group. Keep in mind that if one person has reservations then it is best to not issue an invitation to that person. This preliminary group needs to be in total accord about the list.

Name	Phone	Email	Yes	No

It is desired for each group to have a facilitator – one whose job it is to set meeting dates, send reminders, arrange for a meeting place, assure that there is something on the agenda for each meeting and keep the meeting on track. Ideally this should be someone who is comfortable in a leadership role, or who is just naturally bossy J.

Who will be the facilitator for your group?

Will the same person keep the position or will it be rotating within the group? What will be the timetable for switching if that is what you choose? Who is next on the rotation?

Next is a decision about where the first meeting will be held, as well as date and time. As I suggest in the book, our group found it best to keep the meeting duration limited to no more than two hours. The place should be a home or someplace comfortable and private to facilitate open discussion, as well as being able to accommodate the number of attendees that may be coming. If participants are in different cities or states, plan on setting up a Zoom or Skype with a screen that can be seen by everyone at each location.

Date and Time:

Place (Address and Directions):

Now that you have a list of invitees and a date, time and place for the meeting, next is deciding how you will word the invitation. If by phone or in person, the list can be divided and a basic script can be used to present the idea. If you decide to invite by email, you can send a group bcc email to all the invitees. I suggest that the invitations be done in person or by phone so that everyone is clear in language and tone.

Here is suggested wording, but please discuss and make it your own. If you want to use my wording, of course it is perfectly fine. After initial pleasantries, begin.

"*I have something I want to ask you about. (Name initial group members) got together and we are beginning a lightworkers group. Your name came up as someone we thought may be interested and that we thought would be a good fit. The purpose of the group is spiritual in nature and a way for us to make a difference in the world and all its inhabitants by bringing in more light and positive energy. I'll be happy to answer any questions you have. We have a meeting scheduled for (date and time) and hope you will be able to join us.*"

If yes, give them the particulars about where and, if you're doing a potluck, that they should bring something to eat or drink to share. If no, thank them for considering and close the conversation.

This is the wording we want to use to issue our group invitations:

The first few meetings are going to be focused on getting to know one another and creating a group energy and cohesiveness. Some sort of ritual for opening the meeting is good to mark a beginning to the meeting and to let everyone focus their attention on the group and leave behind whatever thoughts or personal issues they brought in with them.

What will be your opening ritual for this first meeting? The facilitator or the small group can choose this with the knowledge that it can be changed later if need be.

To begin the first meeting, the facilitator should introduce themselves and give a brief overview of why this group is being formed and what the ultimate goals are.

What is the overview and what are the ultimate goals (at least initially) of the group that you wish to present at the first meeting?

Next it is time for the facilitator to go over the basic rules and what conduct is expected. For example, for individual check-in at the beginning of each meeting, let people know what is appropriate to share and for what duration. Let them know this is an update on what is going on in their life and to share anything they wish about their spiritual journey that may have happened since the last meeting. Let people know this is not a time for rants about politics, environmental issues or anything like that — or things that are too personal. It should be emphasized from the beginning that there is no talking from anyone other than the person speaking. If there are questions or comments, they should be saved until that person has finished their update. From the beginning, emphasis should be given that any personal information shared within the group is to remain only in the group and not to be shared with those outside the group unless permission is given.

Meetings will start and end on time. It needs to be expressed that folks should arrive on time if at all possible. Once the meeting has started, it is difficult to maintain the meditative and cohesive state if people are wandering in a few at a time. Life happens and some-times people are going to be late. Let them know that, if possible, they should let another group member know they are coming but will be late, and when they enter, do so quietly and wait until who-ever is speaking has stopped to enter the room and the circle. If someone is going to miss the meeting entirely, they should let the facilitator know so that the group won't be expecting them. Also ascertain if each person is all right with sharing their email and phone information so a group email can be set up, and so people know how to contact each other individually.

These are suggestions. What do you want to let people know at your first meeting?

If the group decides that it would like to include food and drink (alcoholic and/or non-alcoholic) after the meeting, ask the participants what their preferences are and also make note if there are any allergies or dietary restrictions. This can then be shared in a group email so everyone is aware. If people are joining via Zoom or Skype, they can still be online and participate since this is a good time for building group cohesion.

What would your group prefer to do about food and drink after the meeting? List any dietary restrictions and allergies.

Next at this first meeting allow people to tell their individual story (decide a time limit in advance and tell them) of their spiritual journey, why they are interested in this group and what they think they can bring to the group as far as skills or just support and/or enthusiasm.

What are skills or interests are members bringing to the group? This may be helpful to write down for future reference.

Name	Skill	Suggestions

After that part is finished, discuss which days and times are best for the group members to meet. If anyone can suggest another more suitable space to meet, this is also the time for that.

List what days/times/places are suggested and work well for everyone?

Date, time and place for the next and subsequent meetings.

Ending the meetings is another important ritual to formally bring a close to the combined energy of the people in attendance. In our group, the facilitator selects a different person to end the meeting each time. They can have their own way of doing this. We have had prayers, chants, singing, or just simple statements of blessing and gratitude. There is no right or wrong way to do this.

How does your group want to end the meetings?

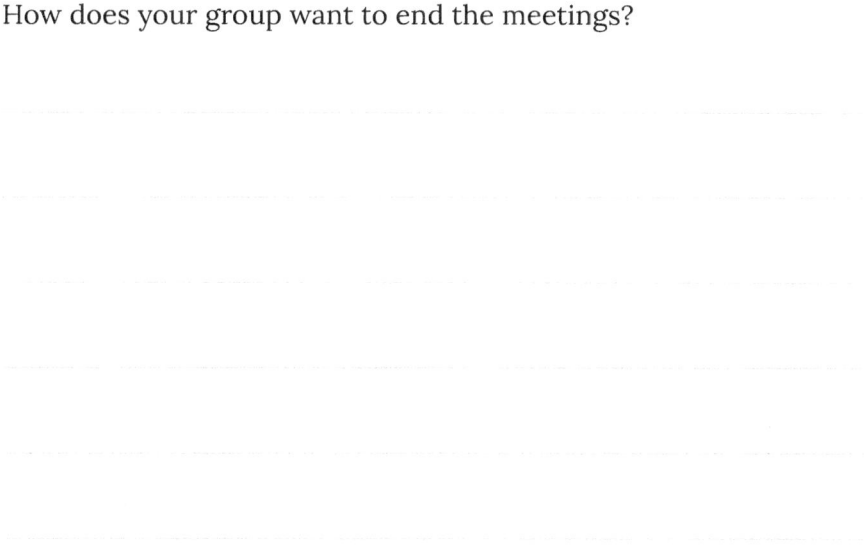

At this time, it is wise to also let people know that if, at any point, they feel that this group is not for them for any reason, there will be no hard feelings and no one will take their leaving personally. They will be released from the group with love and good wishes.

After the first meeting, the facilitator or one or more of the initial small group members should follow up with the attendees to see if they were satisfied with the meeting and if they will be returning. If someone at the first meeting decides it is not for them, it is often easier to tell this to one person rather than the entire group.

Name	Return Y/N	Suggestions

For the second and subsequent meetings, there are suggestions of things to begin with to develop group cohesion.

As a way of group focus, it may be helpful to develop a mission statement. Talk about it, toss in ideas and concepts of what you want to accomplish as a group and what you think needs to be accomplished for humanity, for the Earth, for the universe. Whatever the group comes up with is the beginning of a direction. Note that this mission statement is not necessarily written in stone, it can be changed and updated as the group matures and finds focus.

This was our first mission statement offered as an example: "We are diverse humans with similar experiences with soul planes of giving to somewhere and something. BUT together we want to make a bigger contribution — there is a different level than just with our individual efforts. This is a soul heart love thing."

What is the mission statement for your group?

At the next meetings, your group will be discussion what it wants to do and the direction it wants to proceed. Here are a few suggestions about things to do at your meetings until you get up to speed with your own direction. These exercises help to develop group cohesion and a better understanding of how each person receives or processes information.

~Pick a place in the world where there is a natural disaster, conflict or need of any kind and have a group meditation to send energy to that place and those people.

~Have a group meditation focusing on world peace.

~Focus on a group of endangered animals, plants, trees or places and send energy toward their highest good.

~Spend some group meditation time focusing on sending healing and clarity for the oceans and fresh waters of the Earth.

These are just a few things you can work on, and it may spur you to consider other things. Suggested time for these meditations is 15 to 30 minutes in silence. A discussion can follow about what each person experiences during the meditation. The phone app Insight Timer has a great timing device that sounds a light chime.

What things does your group want to work or focus on?

I am available for Zoom consultations if you feel like your group needs help getting started. My contact information is on my website: janicebaker.net.

Now go and shine your light!